I0084506

The Puzzle of the American Economy

The Puzzle of the American Economy

How Changing Demographics Will Affect Our Future and Influence Our Politics

Mark A. Pisano

BLOOMSBURY ACADEMIC
NEW YORK • LONDON • OXFORD • NEW DELHI • SYDNEY

BLOOMSBURY ACADEMIC
Bloomsbury Publishing Inc
1385 Broadway, New York, NY 10018, USA
50 Bedford Square, London, WC1B 3DP, UK
29 Earlsfort Terrace, Dublin 2, Ireland

BLOOMSBURY, BLOOMSBURY ACADEMIC and the Diana logo are
trademarks of Bloomsbury Publishing Plc

First published in the United States of America by ABC-CLIO 2017
Paperback edition published by Bloomsbury Academic 2024

Copyright © Mark A. Pisano, 2017

For legal purposes the Acknowledgments on p. vii constitute
an extension of this copyright page.

Cover design: Silverander Communications
Cover photo: Map of the United States. (young84/Thinkstock)

All rights reserved. No part of this publication may be reproduced or
transmitted in any form or by any means, electronic or mechanical,
including photocopying, recording, or any information storage or retrieval
system, without prior permission in writing from the publishers.

Bloomsbury Publishing Inc does not have any control over, or responsibility for,
any third-party websites referred to or in this book. All internet addresses given
in this book were correct at the time of going to press. The author and publisher
regret any inconvenience caused if addresses have changed or sites have
ceased to exist, but can accept no responsibility for any such changes.

A catalog record for this book is available from the Library of Congress.

ISBN: HB: 978-1-4408-5310-4
PB: 979-8-7651-3290-6
ePDF: 978-1-4408-5311-1
eBook: 979-8-2161-3461-9

To find out more about our authors and books visit www.bloomsbury.com
and sign up for our newsletters.

Contents

Acknowledgments

The insights to write this book were developed over four decades of association with the Demographic Analysis Unit of the Southern California Association of Governments: 32 years as the executive director of the association and 10 years as a researcher and writer working with the unit. The mission of the association is to develop the long-range plans and policies that will guide the region's physical and economic development. The most useful lens for fulfilling these responsibilities was the demographic work of the unit. Thanks to those who drafted the federal and state directives calling for this work and to the association's local policy board, all 76 local elected officials, who had the courage to adopt and support the work. Most important, thanks to Frank Wen who served as staff director for the past two decades and who assisted me. The work of the unit, the large-scale big data and analytical capacity, provided the contemporary tools to look at the region and the nation differently and to be able to paint this important picture of our economic system. A logical next step was the application to the nation.

My mentor, friend, and racquetball partner Warren Bennis, before his death encouraged me to turn our discussions into a book, noting that he sensed a fundamental change in economic behavior coming. Insights were also obtained from many academic colleagues: David Swanson of the University of California at Riverside, Public Policy School, who encouraged me to look at economics from a demographic perspective; Dowell Meyers of the USC Price School of Public Policy, who encouraged me to present historical demographic data insights before discussing future implications; Dan Mazmanian of the USC Price School of Public Policy, who enabled me to research and write about the relationship between growth and sustainability, environmental and fiscal; Sherry Bebitch Jeffe, my officemate, helped me understand the political implications of these economic changes;

Rich Callahan of the University of San Francisco School of Business and Public Management; and Yan Tang of the USC Price School of Public Policy for the research association on many of the subjects covered in the book.

This book is about the challenges facing the real world today. Insights from boards and staff, such as the National Academy of Public Administration, California Forward—especially Fred Silva; Southwest Megaregion Alliance—especially Bev Perry; and America 2050—especially Bob Yaro provided real-time learning and testing of today's challenges and ideas for the future. In particular, special thanks to Scott Fosler, Paul Posner, and other members of the Federal System Panel who were invaluable colleagues. The practical insights from business boards and advisory boards were the testing ground for many ideas. Particularly helpful were Don Givirtz of Foothill Capital and Tony Morris of AMT Technologies. The complexity of today's world can only come from multiple platforms and disciplines.

Thanks to Clint Gardiner, who assisted and advised me in translating complex economic and demographic ideas into more understandable language; and to Van Gordon Sauter, who consistently encouraged me to help America understand what it faces in clear terms. Finally and most important, without the support, encouragement, listening, and editing assistance of my wife, Jane Pisano, this book would not have been written.

PART 1

Lessons from Demography

CHAPTER ONE

Introduction

When you think of the national economy, what comes to mind? Do you think of the government expenditures and fiscal policy measures pushed by the president and passed by Congress? Would you think of our quarterly GDP growth or annual increases in per capita income? Perhaps you would concentrate instead on the monetary policies and practices of the Federal Reserve, or maybe you would recall a recent article you read about an investigation into a bank or investment firm. And, surely, you would consider tax incentives, the national debt, and balancing the budget. Am I right?

Currently, these are the ideas most of us rely on to sum up the story of our national economy, and all are correct. Yet, even an explanation that included all of these factors would still be fundamentally inadequate and incomplete. What is missing you ask? The answer is . . . *you. Did you know that you, and all the other Americans dispersed throughout the nation, are the very basis of our economy?*

Well, that is what this book is about; it is about *you*, the collective *you*— that is to say, *us*. It is a book about "We the People," not only the theoretical community our founders envisioned with this phrase from our Constitution, but also the actual population of "these United States" established by it. This is a book about our national economy, too, which amounts to saying the same thing, because not only do "We the People" define the economy, but *we are the economy*. We are the basic reason for its existence and the structuring force that gives it shape. We are the most significant cause of its fluctuations and the most significant group these fluctuations affect. As you will see, we are the most predictable pattern underlying these changes, too.

Indeed, "We the People"' of the United States are the very basis of our economy and this book is our story. It is the story of how *We the People* became *We the Economy*; and so in order to tell this story, we will need to focus on ourselves: on who we are, how old we are, how we are changing, and how these individual changes lead to economic change at the national level. Once we accomplish this, we will no longer need to see our national economy as the baffling riddle that so many of our economic experts compare it to. While it is true that many factors legitimately influence the economy and complicate our picture of it, we have mostly looked for answers in the wrong places: Wall Street, Main Street, the White House, to name a few. All the while, the most significant key to understanding the economy remained hidden from our view. We did not see it because our eyes were focused in the wrong direction.

The purpose of this book is to shift the direction of our line of sight. We should not waste any more time looking out there for someone to blame for our problems—immigrants, Obama, Wall Street executives. We need to look within—that is, we need *insight*. For only by acknowledging our role in our own story will we begin to understand an economy that baffles even our top experts. We will come to agree with Socrates that self-knowledge is the key to wisdom. By understanding how all of us collectively contribute to the economy and how these contributions change rapidly over time, we will develop a clear lens to look at our situation as a nation. Only then can we develop an effective method to evaluate the solutions proposed by our public servants; only then can we play our rightful role in the economy.

This aim does not imply, however, that our current financial situation will be easy to explain or that the upcoming challenges we face as a nation will be easy to solve. Nothing could be further from the truth. Not only is the United States home to 324 million residents and the "single largest national economy" in the world "with a per capita GDP [gross domestic product] of $54,800" and a total annual income of well over $18 trillion; but, more important, it is currently emitting a confusing mix of contradictory messages. For this reason, it is not surprising that several writers compared our national economy to a riddle, a puzzle, or other metaphors implying complexity, difficulty, and mystery. When subject matter approaches maximum complexity, we tend to use metaphors to describe it. Speaking figuratively, the U.S. economy is like a vast labyrinth where every path branches off to a different individual, business, organization, or government involved in the production, distribution, and consumption of all U.S. goods and services. The labyrinth is very difficult to map in detail, not only because it is so vast but also because every path within it is in constant fluctuation and realignment. Like all great labyrinths, this one has a minotaur at the center of it. In our story, the monster's name is Recession and he likes to ask riddles. If you answer correctly, you have a chance at survival as long as you can find your way out of the labyrinth. Recession, the bull-headed monster, wants to know the following: what is the one element that no economy can exist without but is shrinking in the wrong place in the United States? If you answered money, sorry, economies have existed without money (the barter system), and the United States has more cash than it ever has before. If you want to know the correct answer, then you will have to read the book.

Perhaps the reference to a classical myth has you thinking that you are about to read the work of another professor obsessed with the latest academic trend, that new obsession with how to look at history and at changes in economies and political systems. Although it is true that population changes can explain the collapse of many ancient empires (Greece, Rome, Constantinople, among others), this is not my main purpose. I will provide a method for understanding what is happening right now, not only because present circumstances are what concern us most, but also because our history lessons no longer apply. We have reached a turning point in history, a period of unprecedented change. If you were to browse through the titles of headlines from the front page of any major newspaper over the past 50 years, it would become immediately clear that not only have times changed, but the rate at which events occur in time also has changed.

The economic changes that we encounter today occur at a speed and on a scale that would previously have been inconceivable. What took centuries to occur in the past now happen over the course of decades. In terms of technology alone, more change occurred in the last century than in all the centuries of the last millennium combined. Winston Churchill, for instance, rode a horse into battle and lived to see a rocket travel to outer space. As it relates to this book, the dawn of the Information Age or the Global Ages (call it what you will)—that period since 1950 when the world population tripled and GDP multiplied six-fold, the cumulative effects of rapid advancements in communications and information technologies, along with huge leaps in agriculture, education, medicine, transportation, and war—dramatically transformed the world. The increase in urbanization, the return of pluralism, the expansion of the nation-state, the globalization of communication systems and financial markets, the success of capitalism and the failure of communism, the proliferation of nuclear weapons, and the birth of new threats like cyberterrorism have all dramatically affected us and will continue to have long-term impacts on the global economy. To ignore the effects of these changes today would only invite disaster for tomorrow.

The best way to look at change on a massive scale is by examining empirical evidence. It is crucial, however, that we first put our old ideas aside, for nothing poses a larger obstacle to discovering truth than the belief that we know about a topic prior to investigating it. We are all familiar with demographics from the world of politics, primarily as a point of reference for elections. During a year of campaign strategies, presidential election predictions, and surprising election results it is hardly an exaggeration to say that it is impossible to turn on the news without encountering an exhaustive examination of the American people as a population of voters. Why should we not use the same type of data that politically astute campaign managers have been using to their advantage for the past 50 years? It is crucial that we apply the demographic method to a larger and more influential subject, one in which small variations do not lead to the distortions and poor predictions we sometimes see in election analysis. For in a capitalist society, the largest and most significant level of understanding is economic; and the best way to understand this level is through the analysis of statistical data. Since "We the People" are both the greatest source of economic change and the ultimate context in which it occurs, the most accurate method that we may employ to understand ourselves is demographics.

CHAPTER TWO

"The Wonderful, Terrible, Inscrutable Economy"

Did the latest news stories about the presidential election of 2016 leave you scratching your head in wonder or shaking it in dismay? Do you ever find yourself bewildered by the sheer size of the numbers that policy makers and journalists mention nonchalantly when reporting bank bailouts or the national debt? Are you finding it increasingly difficult to isolate the facts from the barrage of contradictory statements made by the political candidates? Did you ever wonder when listening to some of the candidates talk about their plans, if the individual in question is deliberately lying or just misinformed? If you answered yes to any of the preceding questions, you are not alone, and you need not fear. You are having a normal response to an abnormal situation. Listening to the 2016 presidential candidates' plans to improve the economy (when they *had* plans) was like taking a trip to a Land of Economic Confusion.

Most Americans are confused and many feel left behind. According to a Gallup poll conducted on April 14, 2016, an overwhelming majority of Americans listed the economy as their number one concern, and 71 percent said that they were dissatisfied with our "country's direction." This sentiment continued throughout the election and was a determinate factor in the elections results, particularly in the rust belt swing states. Our two major political parties clearly took the collective dissatisfaction into account, which resulted in a "negative flavor" during the election cycle. The most popular candidates in the primaries were those who seemed the most frustrated with the economy and other related hot button issues, such as the labor market, immigration, and the minimum wage. While the Republican Party has certainly emphasized anger more than the Democratic Party, it is interesting that the Democratic candidates have not made more of the economic progress of the last few years, or at least taken credit for many of the successes proclaimed by the incumbent administration. Despite whatever else we may think of them, the men and women who manage the recent election campaigns know how to use demographics to their advantage.

Evaluating this year's campaigns for the presidential nomination, when judged by the standards of their intended purpose, leaves a sense of missed opportunity. The purpose of the campaigns for the presidential nomination is to provide the American people with the opportunity to learn about each candidate's experience, ethical values, leadership qualities, domestic and foreign policy, and vision for the future. The campaigns from the primaries through the general election are, in effect, a series of televised job interviews to decide the next president of the United States—that is, our head of state, the highest-ranking federal officer in the executive branch, and the commander-in-chief of the United States Armed Forces, the most powerful military force on Earth.

Most days we do not have time to think this deeply about it. While the media circus plays in the background of our lives, we are busy trying to navigate the real storms of loss and gain that define today's market. If your life is anything like most Americans', then you know what it means to live with financial insecurity: to worry about how to make ends meet and keep the wolves at the door at bay. You know the meaning of uncertainty: to wonder if anyone will hire you again, if you will lose the house or get the loan, or if you will make it until midnight when your paycheck clears.

When did keeping our heads above water become the sole objective? An average weekday in the life of most Americans is hectic. Practically every day, each of us is required to make stressful decisions with our hard-earned money. Whether we are trying to purchase a home or car, pay for skyrocketing costs of education, or put away money for our retirement, this uncertainty leads to confusion and even anger when we hear the words used by most politicians, whether already in office or seeking it. We wonder how their recommendations could help us. If their description of the economy does not match our experience, then what can we do to help ourselves?

First, we need to make sense of this perplexing puzzle. We need to identify the nature of the problem before we can find strategies to solve it, if any exist. Perhaps we are beginning to doubt even this. No, we must believe solutions exist. We are Americans; after all; we invented second chances. Did not most of our ancestors come here for this exact reason? Immigrants still perceive the United States as a land of opportunity, although many

Americans resent this now. What ever happened to "give us your hungry, your tired, your poor, your huddled masses"? When the Pilgrims and Puritans arrived in the seventeenth century, this land represented a second chance, a fresh start for those fleeing starvation, disease, persecution, poverty, and war. While not all immigrants came to the United States under such dramatic circumstances and some came under worse ones—exile, indentured servitude, or slavery—almost every person here is an immigrant or a child of immigrants.

Besides, nearly all of us (adults, at least) know the true meaning of a second chance. At some point in our lives, each of us has faced adversity, survived, and started over. Whether this trouble came in the form of job loss, business failure, unfavorable legal judgment, divorce, foreclosure, bankruptcy, a life-threatening illness, or the death of a parent or spouse, we know how to pick up the pieces, set new goals, and start again. For these reasons, we are as certain that there are solutions to our financial problems as we are of death and taxes. The good news is that any problem with our national economy, by definition, is not a burden carried alone.

As any mathematician will tell you, the first step in problem solving is to identify the problem. In order to accomplish this, we will need to clear away the muddled thinking and political biases that surround the economy. Next, we need to assess the situation, paying particularly close attention to our role in the economy. Granted, it is not easy to explore our dilemma in detail in a nation of 324 million people, but it is possible nonetheless. So let us begin by asking ourselves, what economic realities are we actually facing?

A wise place to start would be to explore and examine the official account of the events of the past decade.

From the Great Recession to the Present

The Great Recession, the worst economic decline since the Great Depression of the 1930s, officially began at the end of 2007 and lasted until at least the middle of 2009. In the United States, we classify an economy as in recession when the gross domestic product (GDP) drops for two consecutive quarters. In 2006, for example, the GDP averaged approximately 1 percent growth every quarter; whereas in 2007, our GDP started shrinking each quarterly period and, by the end of the fourth quarter officially sank into a recession that lasted through the second quarter of 2009. It is misleading to say our economic decline ended after only four quarters of negative growth, however, since the United States showed almost no signs of recovery until 2010. Furthermore, according to the International Monetary Fund

(IMF), a major recession continued globally for another six months. Incidentally, the IMF does not base its criteria for classifying a recession on a specific amount of time the GDP wanes; instead, it uses a combination of macroeconomic indicators (e.g., capital flows, employment rates, GDP, etc.) for however long is necessary to determine a pattern of decline, which is a good example of the use of quantitative data advocated in this book.

Speaking of data, the reason demographics are more accurate and thus better served studying the national economy than predicting presidential primaries is the Law of Large Numbers (also known as the Law of Averages), which states that as the number of events we are measuring gets larger, the percentage difference between the expected outcome and the actual outcome decreases. Demographic-economic forecasts, even long-run forecasts, are accurate for this reason. The United States is a perfect candidate for this type of analysis because our total wealth and resources are more like a small planet than a country. In fact, some of our states have larger economies than the largest nation-states in Europe. The state of California, for example, was the sixth largest economy in the world in 2016 placing it above Italy, Canada, Australia, South Korea, and Spain. When you consider that in order to calculate our national income, you have to add California's GDP to the GDP of 49 other states, it becomes clear why the Law of Large Numbers works greatly in our favor.

To examine the narrative that most economists provide to explain the Great Recession, we need to step back to the turn of the millennium, when many of America's largest financial institutions sold mortgage-backed securities (MBSs) with deceptive financial instruments (derivatives) tied to them. At first, this caused the value of houses to spike upward, creating an $8 trillion housing bubble. When thousands of homeowners could not repay their loans due to these toxic mortgages, however, the bubble burst in December 2007. As the value of homes rapidly imploded, the subsequent equity market fluctuations caused a massive loss of personal wealth (not billions but *trillions* of dollars). Consumer confidence was at its lowest level in decades, and a sharp decline in consumer spending and business investment followed. The value of stocks, bonds, and securities plummeted, which further exacerbated the massive cutbacks in business investments and consumer spending, and accelerated the downward spiral. Soon thereafter, we found ourselves in the midst of a global credit crisis when the most powerful financial institutions in the United States and Europe nearly went bankrupt. When one of the oldest and most highly respected firms, Lehman Brothers, filed for Chapter 11 on September 15, 2008, the consequences reverberated across the globe, triggering severe losses here and abroad. The Dow Jones closed with a loss at barely above 500 points that day, which was at the time the largest stock market drop in a single day since the terrorist attacks of September 11, 2001.

Doomsday prophets began to appear in every newspaper and on radio and television programs warning us of the financial apocalypse that was coming. If the failure of a single institution like Lehman Brothers could harm the market in this manner, then the bankruptcy of any of the significantly larger financial institutions (or a handful of the midsized ones), would surely initiate the downfall of our economy and the ruin of any other nation deeply invested in our success. We could not afford any more bankruptcies, we were told, because these companies were simply "too big to fail," and a new phrase entered the everyday lexicon of the American people. President Bush and Congress immediately sprang into action: authorizing strong and swift fiscal and monetary measures requiring the Federal Reserve to establish a series of programs that offered tens to hundreds of billions of dollars in credit to each institution deemed "too big to fail."

In the months before President Obama took office in 2008, the "economy was shrinking at a rate of over 8 percent, 800 thousand jobs were lost a month, banks would not lend to families and small businesses," and the American auto industry, the last monument of American manufacturing, was on the brink of collapse.[1] The Great Recession that began on Main Street was now a global financial crisis that ultimately cost millions of Americans their jobs, their homes, and their savings. By the end of the recession, the U.S. labor market reported a loss of 8.4 million jobs from the start of 2008 to the end of 2009.[2]

We emerged from this crisis under the assumption that by correcting the overleveraging of our financial excesses and debts, public and private, we would stabilize the market and get back to our main objective: economic growth. Members of both parties congratulated one another on discovering the source of our downfall: the excesses of Fannie Mae and Freddie Mac, the banks and mortgage companies. In February 2008, the Obama administration, with the support of Congress, attempted to revive the depressed economy with an "economic stimulus package"—namely, the American Recovery and Reinvestment Act, a massive spending bill initially estimated at $787 billion but later revised to $831 billion in 2009. As a single-expenditure item, this bill was unprecedented; in fact, it was the largest spending program (outside military expenditures) in our nation's history. Yet it demonstrated the ability of our political leadership to come together and deal with a crisis facing the country, precisely when their willingness to do so was becoming questionable. "Too big to fail" regulatory policies were legislated, implemented, and executed so that these colossal firms could not take us hostage and force us to bail them out ever again.

The last leg on the so-called three-legged stool of our economic recovery and stimulus policy was the Federal Reserve's lowering the interest rate that the central bank charges its members. Led by Ben Bernanke, this policy was meant to stimulate investment in our country. A few years later, Bernanke and his successor, Janet Yellen, initiated a new approach to monetary policy, Quantitative Easing, which purchased large amounts of debt and had the overall effect of adding $4.48 trillion into the U.S. economy.[3] Instead of printing money, which would increase the balance sheet of the Federal Reserve (i.e., increase their liabilities), money that was already in circulation, particularly troubled assets were purchased by the Federal Reserve and used to leverage the economy. The two-pronged policy of easy money and low interest (actually, zero interest) was supposed to propel the economy forward, the intended consequences of which would be job growth, reduction of the unemployment rate, and an increase in wages paid. Accompanying this stimulated market activity would be some inflationary activity, targeted at a 2 percent rate. The challenge for the Federal Reserve was to balance this seesaw as we continued to place more and more weight on the debit side.

Bold corrective actions were needed and taken—for example, the Dodd-Frank reforms—but up to now, here are the results: after almost a decade, the large banks are even larger and the smaller banks have been disappearing.

The United States muddled through six years of recovery with much fanfare over the numbers of jobs created and the corresponding decrease in the unemployment rate. Despite the official party line taken by the Obama administration, the labor market improved at a painfully slow pace. Furthermore, when we closely examine the demographic data, a very different picture of our unemployment rate begins to emerge. "Labor force participation," a term that refers to the percentage of the population who are of working age and actually working, is at the historically low rate of 62.4 percent. To put matters into perspective, this means that less than two-thirds of the population between the ages 18 and 65 is employed. Labor force participation has not been this low in 40 years.[4]

The three-legged stool of the Great Recession—a massive fiscal expenditure focused on public works and low-interest assistance to financial institutions, regulatory policies focused on those firms considered too big to fail, and super-low interest rates, coupled with huge injections of money—was aimed at stimulating the economy. The fact is, most Americans are not aware that their role in the economy is of greater importance than any captain of industry.

It is time to take a twenty-first-century view of the problem. Only then will we be in the position to offer viable strategies to address our economic predicament. As you will see in the next chapter, the consumer is in charge of global commerce now; the consumer decides which companies will thrive and which will perish. The only entity truly too big to fail is the American people.

The Current Economic Puzzle

The first 10 days of 2016 were the worst start of the stock market in over a century, and the month ended with a 5.5 percent drop in value.[5] Business investment barely grew a meager 2 percent in 2015, the lowest growth since the start of the Great Recession. What force(s) drive these numbers? Why has it taken longer to recover than any other recession to date? We were back to business as usual after only a few years following the burst of the Internet bubble, yet it has been nine years after the housing market crash and six years since even the most conservative economists considered us in a recession. Several ominous signals appeared in some of the world's largest markets since the start of 2016, including a remarkable decline in investments in infrastructure and other tangible fixed assets, such as major plants and equipment, and even in traditional energy markets where the United States would ultimately emerge as the world's leading supplier, though not without a cost.

Meanwhile, an unknown force has decelerated the economic recovery of many of the world's largest national economies, including Japan, China, the Eurozone, Brazil, Russia, and some countries in the Middle East. The subdued recovery of the global economy has impacted the United States in a variety of ways, ranging from significant drops in commodity prices to the overall decline of two of the most highly valued industries of the past: manufacturing and agriculture.

Looking at one commodity more closely is illustrative. The price of soybeans that earned $18 a bushel in 2012 has gradually declined in value. At the start of 2016, the price was $8.90 a bushel. Now imagine you have invested heavily in this commodity. Can you really handle more than a 50 percent reduction in the value of your investment in less than three and a half years? Worse, imagine you are a soybean farmer: can you handle making over 50 percent less on your main crop than you made just few years ago? Hypothetically, if a soybean farmer's net farm income was $90,000 last year (pretty close to the median), this year his net was just over $45,000. Can any of us really afford to make 50 percent less than we did three years ago? Let us say your household income was $60,000 at the end of 2012 (pretty close to the median family income that year), and suddenly you are asked to survive on $30,000 a year. How would you pull it off? If you were buying a house, you probably just lost it. If you were renting an apartment, you now need to move to a smaller apartment. Moreover, you can definitely forget about acquiring anything "extra" this year. Whether you had planned on buying a new car, going on vacation, hiring a tutor for your child, assisting a relative pay for an expensive medical treatment, or retiring a year early to get to know your grandkids better—all of those plans, no matter how noble in intent or how important to you, just vanished like a dream. Many Americans found themselves in similar circumstances *after* the recession. Our economy is the result of the countless stories of how we are dealing with these changes over time.

Proponents of the "U.S. economy is as resilient as ever" school of thought might argue that commodity prices are improving. As of May 22, 2016, for example, soybeans were up to $10.66 a bushel. To these optimists we could only respond: is a 40 percent reduction of net income really that much easier to live on? Furthermore, soybeans were not the only commodity to fall. Steel and equipment commodities had similar declines and similar results nationwide. Critics may argue that commodity fluctuations are the unfortunate by-product of free enterprise and always occur regardless of the health of the national economy. But there is legitimate cause for concern when multiple markets are in steady decline worldwide and we call this a "recovery."

This scenario is, in fact, the current situation, but it is not the whole story. The optimists are not entirely wrong, but neither are those who argue that we need to start preparing for another economic downturn, as we will see. The energy markets are a good example of this fundamental ambiguity. As the result of technological innovation, price, and policy considerations, our country vaulted into the position of the world's leading supplier of energy. Since the largest energy commodity is still oil, this was surprising. For those who have not followed this story closely, suffice to say we are the world's leading consumer of energy, particularly oil, which we primarily obtained from foreign countries until just a few years ago. For the first time in recent history we relied more on domestic production of oil than foreign sources. Second, we have dominated many markets, but it has been difficult to produce more oil than Russia. From a purely economic view (i.e., leaving out environmental considerations), this qualifies as one of the greatest, though least publicized, accomplishments of the Obama administration. Our dependence on foreign oil has decreased every year President Obama has been office until finally we began to rely more on domestic than foreign oil.

For those of us who have watched our dependency on foreign oil grow over the years, while our military conflicts with some of the more belligerent nations and terrorist organizations in the Middle East appeared to escalate, this seemed like a miracle.

The surprises did not stop there, however. Energy markets continued to decline even though we became the world's leading supplier of energy. Traditionally, a decline in oil prices always leads to economic growth. Yet oil prices have reduced to levels that we have not seen since 2003 (with prices dropping from $100 to $30 a barrel and then rising to $50 a barrel) without providing any benefit to the American economy. In the past, consumers would take advantage of low oil prices by filling their gas tanks, more often for less money without harming American companies. Now that the oil is mostly produced here, however, the amount of actual demand did not meet the expected demands, and we ended up with a market flooded with an overabundant supply of cheap oil. Why Americans are buying less oil despite the fact that in some areas the price has dropped 50 percent is unclear. The gradual change to renewable energies resulting from policies to deal with environmental issues and the rise in the production of natural gas resulting from new technologies have certainly contributed but cannot account for the decrease in demand. Are Americans still weary or resentful of the prices offered during the Great Recession? Are we still too far in debt to seize on new opportunities to save money at the gas pump? Whatever the case, this surprising disappointment in domestic sales hit energy companies hard and resulted in cutbacks in investment and massive layoffs, while the gains we expected never arrived.

The Unemployment Level

In spite of all these warning signals, the predictions of some of our more optimistic economists seemed to hold true, as the U.S. economy remained resilient throughout the year. We enjoyed three years of job growth, replaced the jobs lost in the Great Recession, and reduced the level of unemployment by over 50 percent (from the recessionary level of 10 percent to 4.6 percent). Policy makers continued to debate what the real level of unemployment in our country is as the actual number of Americans who did not participate in legal full-time employment continued unabated. Those who pointed out that Americans were out of work for a longer period than previous recessions did not find much evidence to contradict their views. Others supported this argument by pointing to the substantial expansion of the safety net: increases in food stamps, health benefits, government-paid cell phones, and more assistance to families with dependents clearly indicated that the welfare state was growing as rapidly as the employment numbers decreased. Some argued that these handouts had reached such a high level that people were actually discouraged from looking for work, as many jobs did not provide the benefits available through these programs. As the slow recovery dragged on and employers continued posting job needs, the number of unfilled jobs began to grow, which demonstrated either that the skills of our workforce were not well matched for our economy or that the unemployed had given up looking for work. The truth is our current definitions of unemployment cannot account for the reasons underlying the fact of our low labor force participation numbers. Whether this fact is due to the lack of skills, the loss of confidence, the perceived benefits of remaining on welfare, or the rise in "under the table" or illegal employment remains unclear at this time.

What is clear, however, is that 85 percent of the jobs created during the recovery period were in the lower-paying service sector, which added to income inequality, accelerated the disintegration of the middle class, and widened the gap between rich and poor, the most serious economic issue America faces today.[6] The problem is that current wages when adjusted for inflation are virtually the same as they were in 2006 with a slight increase occurring recently. Manufacturing accounts for only 9 percent of employment, and the mixed growth in the construction industry contributed to the financial slump. Median household incomes over the recovery period, when adjusted for inflation, fell by nearly 6.5 percent. More problematic than the decline during a period of recovery was the distribution of these income reductions. Young people ages 15–24 showed the largest decline in income, over 15 percent, while seniors (65 and older) had an increase in average annual incomes, reporting income gains over 5 percent. The disparity here marks an intergenerational difference of 20 percent from past levels. Middle-age people 45–54 had the next largest decline in incomes, over 9 percent; followed by foreign-born immigrants, 8 percent.[7] Last, Americans who lived below the poverty level grew more numerous, to 42.6 million, with 44.3 percent of them having less than half the income to escape the poverty level (a cautionary note: census data do not include income received from safety net programs).

Yet the ambiguity continued because GDP grew at 2 percent this past year, keeping up with the average pace of growth over the past few years and keeping us well above the negative growth required to be deemed in a recession, yet nevertheless substantially less than in the decade prior to the recession. This is not the level needed to create new opportunities and grow the economy. Finally, the intended goal of increasing the rate of inflation to meet the target of 2 percent has not been achieved.

Upon analyzing all the data points, we encounter an economy that is confusing, to say the least; an economy that emits mixed signals—strong and weak, improving and worsening, filled with surprising gains and even more surprising losses; an economy that indicates recovery while simultaneously denying it; an economy of paradox and uncertainty; a "terrible, wonderful, and inscrutable economy," as Neil Irwin wrote in the *New York Times*.[8] The humbling truth that few economists or politicians have the courage to admit is that no one really knows what to do about this. Even the Federal Reserve Bank is baffled as to what further stimulus programs they could offer to hit the target 2 percent inflation, reduce the unemployment rate, and increase the wages that have steadily declined in value over the past several years. There is not much more they can do with the interest rate hovering just above 0 percent and an overabundance of money already injected into the economy—and there is even disagreement on this. How do we get to higher GDP growth levels, or, to put it in more frightening terms, how do we avoid falling back into another recession?

The enigma of our past and current economic decline persists as the threat of another recession looms on the horizon. The mystery of our economy remains at the center of our national concerns and in the eye of the storm of our political debates. The daily crossfire between the Democratic presidential administration and the Republican Congress has emphasized our past, current, and future financial state. Indeed, it could be said that the weapon of choice of both parties is blaming one another for our current financial predicament. The confusion as to the actual state of the economy and how to resolve the dilemmas facing the populace has grown because of misinformation, political grandstanding, and exaggerations presented on both sides. Sadly, the 2016 presidential campaigns did little but further divide an already fragmented country. All seventeen of the Republican candidates railed against high government spending, the ever-increasing $18 trillion debt, and the $544 billion added to this debt in 2016. The increasing size of our national debt seems to be the only element of our economy whose growth we can actually rely on each year. If America continues in this manner, our national debt will reach $26 trillion by 2024.[9] These debts piled on, one after the other, are added to an already overburdened economy whose sluggish growth is encumbered by debt, high taxes, financial regulations, and a lack of employment opportunities.

Democratic candidates joined the Republicans in criticizing the economy, noting the lack of job opportunities for young people. They decried the income gains of the very wealthiest of Americans and criticized the growing gap between rich and poor. Some Democrats went so far as to claim that the economy is rigged against the poor and middle class. While it is not unusual for candidates to be critical of the current state of affairs, particularly as far as the economy is concerned, the most startling and disturbing aspect of the 2016 election season was the bitterness and rage directed at the establishment by Democrats and Republicans alike. The opinions of voters were highly negative against "establishment" candidates—or, more accurately, perceived "establishment" candidates. Exit interviews of voters, whose numbers were atypically high in turnout this year, painted a picture of bitter anger aimed at immigrants, high-income individuals, and practically anyone deemed part of "the system." The vitriol of some of the candidates and the surprising support for them by American voters clearly reflected the national frustration with our inability to escape economic decline and the desire to place the blame on a single group or individual we could find responsible for our financial insecurity. It appears that the social contract in America, where we balance individual entrepreneurial desires with the public good, is waning, if not disappearing outright. This is the sad reality of the current state of affairs we must overcome if there is to be any hope of moving the country on a more productive course to address our economic decline.

Four key questions still remain: First, do "We the People" have the collective backbone and will to resolve the polarization of our two leading political parties, and the fragmentations occurring within each? Second, are there underlying changes occurring in America that contribute to the confusing paradoxes of our national economy and the bitter hostility encountered at exit polls? Third, if we can wade through the muddled thinking surrounding this issue, will we be any closer to uncovering the identity of the shadowy force that seems to subdue our recovery and pull us into another recession? Fourth, if we can identify this force, will it clarify matters enough to develop alternative strategies to solve our financial problems?

The next few chapters will examine the possible causes of the predicament so rarely mentioned by our experts. We will see how the dynamics that produce our economy are much more connected to each of us than we now understand. Recognition of these forces and the influences we all have over them should, at the very least, provide us with the necessary foundation on which a framework of economic solutions can be built that will lead to renewed social cohesion.

Notes

1. "The Financial Crisis: Five Years Later—The White House," May 12, 2016, https://www.whitehouse.gov/sites/default/files/docs/20130915-financial-crisis-five-years-later.pdf.

2. "The Great Recession: State of Working America," April 17, 2016, http://stateofworkingamerica.org/great-recession/.

3. Neil Irwin, "Quantitative Easing Is about to End: Here's What It Did in Charts," *New York Times*, October 10, 2014, http://www.nytimes.com/2014/10/30/upshot/quantitative-easing-is-about-to-end-heres-what-it-did-in-seven-charts.html.

4. "United States Labor Force Participation Rate 1950–2016" Trading Places, http://www.tradingeconomics.com/united-states/labor-force-participation-rate.

5. Dana Cimilluca and Saumya Vaishampayan, "Global Stocks Sink on Fresh Growth Fears," *Wall Street Journal*, January, 21, 2016, p. A1, http://www.wsj.com/articles/global-stocks-sink-on-fresh-growth-fears-1453326452.

6. Drew Desilver, "U.S. income inequality, on rise for decades, is now highest since 1928," Pew Center for Research, December 5, 2013, http://www.pewresearch.org/fact-tank/2013/12/05/u-s-income-inequality-on-rise-for-decades-is-now-highest-since-1928/.

7. Jason Deparle and Sabrina Tavernise, "Poor Are Still Getting Poorer, but Downturns' Punch Varies, Census Data Show," *New York Times*, September 15, 2011, p. A24, http://www.nytimes.com/2011/09/15/us/poor-are-still-getting-poorer-but-downturns-punch-varies-census-data-show.html.

8. Neil Irwin, "The, Terrible, Wonderful, Inscrutable Economy," *New York Times*, November 1, 2015, p. B3, http://www.nytimes.com/2015/11/01/upshot/is-the-economy-really-in-trouble.html.

9. "The Deficit Rises Again," *Wall Street Journal*, January 26, 2016, p. A12, http://www.wsj.com/articles/the-deficit-rises-again-1453768153.

CHAPTER THREE

Historical Change, Economic Behavior, and Demographics

Major Transformations

Peter Drucker, in a brief opinion piece published in the *Wall Street Journal*, warned that the greatest challenge of this century would be the reemergence of pluralism as a model for the distribution of power in the political process.[1] Pluralism results when individuals, as opposed to centralized governments, possess the authority and power to effect political and economic change. The conflict between monism and pluralism as political philosophy has been at the heart of American democracy since we declared ourselves independent from the British Empire. From the foundation of the Confederation of States in the Articles that preceded the U.S. Constitution until the fall of imperialism in the last century, pluralism was the clear loser in the conflict between pluralism and monism. We actually carry proof of monism's victory in our wallets. Emblazoned in Latin on the dollar bill are the words "e pluribus unum" (*out of many, one*). Pluralism continued to decline as the United States and other imperial powers competed for world domination in the nineteenth and part of the twentieth century. Shortly after the fall of the Nazi party and its members' dream of a homogenous society consisting of one superrace, the next era, the Information Age or Digital Revolution, caused a reemergence of pluralism. According to Drucker, rapid advances in technology and innovation unleashed the power and influence of the individual on the economy. This is not to say that every centralizing tendency vanished overnight. Even as colonialism disintegrated during the last century, other monistic values remained, such as unilateralism and elitism. Nevertheless, today pluralism clearly has the upper hand in the struggle against its antithesis.

How could the Information Age cause a commercial, social, and political shift of this magnitude? According to Drucker, technology has transformed the focus of the global economy and provided individuals with the agency and authority to determine their own destiny. Not only is the Age of Empires gone, but also even more highly integrated sovereign powers like nation-states no longer determine the destiny of the individuals who live under their authority.

Drucker believes that these technological advances made mental activity and intellectual creativity the driving forces of economic activity, rather than the physical labor inherent in traditional industries such as agriculture and manufacturing. As a result, U.S. commerce has shifted its emphasis from the trade of traditional goods, such as crops and manufactured products, to intellectual properties such as ideas, information, and inventions. Drucker also noted that this shift in emphasis about the nature of production would result in political and economic systems engaging in battles to determine which nation could best deal with these new business opportunities. The trade of information and data as a new economic platform and opportunity for national economic growth, Drucker warns, will be the driving force of the wars of the twenty-first century.

Phillip Bobbitt fleshed out the dimensions of this war in *Shield of Achilles: War, Peace, and the Course of History*,[2] an ambitious and erudite discourse on six centuries of political systems culminating in a dark vision of history and an even darker prognostication of the century to come. Bobbitt described three philosophies of economics employed by the major political powers vying for power and world domination for the duration of modern history: European mercantilism, China's managed economy, and United States' entrepreneurialism. Bobbitt's dynamic view of history suggests that the forces underlying change (both beneficial and destructive) are economic policies, international trade agreements, and political values. For example, one of the tragic ironies of history is that the typical outcome of leaving economic problems unresolved is war, which, in the aftermath, forces changes on the political system that nullify the possible economic solutions to the problem. When we apply this vision to the disruptive forces in the Middle East, particularly radical terrorist organizations and their national sponsors, it becomes clear that our national security is contingent on a detailed analysis of the undercurrents driving our economy and the application of viable solutions to resolve them.

A close examination of these forces reveals that this competition for power, beginning in the first half of the past century, reached a critical mass, and the chain reaction that followed has shaken the foundation of both our national and global economies. In the past few decades, trade agreements led to the globalization of many markets and the emergence of many new ones. Our understanding of these trade agreements and the policy debates surrounding them tend to focus strictly on corporations and the production side of the economy. Noting the difficulties caused by these agreements for American businesses, and the loss of production sites and employment opportunities to other countries, the national conversation also includes the positive effects of reducing the price of goods and increasing the standard of living for most people.

For the past decades, the advantage of improving the standard of living has moved the nation toward more free and open trade. The national dialogue has missed possibly the most important result of what trade has accomplished in the United States and other nations, however—namely the shift in the fundamental roles of who makes economic decisions and who the subject of economic policy should be. More specifically, the most significant consequence of the Global Age is the shift in authority and power from those who control the means of production to those who consume the goods and services created by these means. Through the rapid development of communication, information, and transportation technologies, the world has completely changed in the last 50 years and the economy along with it. Instead of a group of a few hundred companies that control the financial realm, the ruling economic powers are everywhere, and we can shop in any market with a push of a few buttons on our smartphones. As economic beings, we transcend the limits posed by the borders of our cities, counties, states, regions, and nations and thus are not beholden anymore to the whims of the leaders who rule at each level. We are shoppers in a global marketplace where a consumer can purchase goods and services from anywhere in the world at any time of day. Paradoxically, as the reaches of these new markets have grown in size and scope, our sense of the Earth's magnitude has shrunk into the size of our smartphones. Today you can buy a product from China and another from Nebraska in the same hour in an online store like Amazon or a global marketplace like eBay. Or, if you do not like either of those companies, you can easily boycott them without sacrificing the enjoyment of your favorite products. We rarely encounter situations where the rarity of an item limits our selection of which company we need to contact anymore.

Phillip Bobbitt in *Achilles* frames this change perfectly when he observes that the consumer is the new king and de facto decision maker who sits at the head of the economic roundtable that we call the global economy. The former economic ruling class—the presidents and CEOs, the owners and

operators of the producers of goods and services, and the state policymak-
ers governing them—no longer dictate our ability to purchase what we
desire. Consequently, both the nation-state and the producer become sec-
ondary to the individual consumers who use their goods and services. The
phrase "the customer is always right" is no longer solely a customer relations theory, but rather the actual collective reality of the contemporary
world. The genie is now out of the bottle. In a world of connected communication and information, there may be temporary interruptions. We are
now experiencing large Corporations with large cash accumulations fight-
ing back by attempting to consolidate increasing market share through complex management structures that attempt to limit consumer choices.
Time-Warner's attempt to corner the market on the distribution of the *Los
Angeles Dodgers* and force other cable companies to pay large bundling fees
and force viewers to switch their cable services is an example of this continual struggle to control pluralism- but empowered individuals will not
be denied especially in the United States of America that values freedom
of choice as a basic value and a constitutional right.

The changing economic realities we are encountering represent, as Douglass C. North observes, a fundamental shift in the rules of the game for
how the business organizations in our society work.[3] His Nobel Prize–
winning work represents another fundamental shift in our perception of
economics. Fundamental shifts occur in the economy because of changes
in society that are based on fundamental changes in informal rules (behavior or cultural forces such as the rise of the Global Information Age) and
formal rules (for example, changes brought about by trade agreements and
treaties among nations). This time the view of our economic activity is
dependent on the need to meet consumer utility and satisfaction. It is derived
from a global marketplace, not a domestically oriented, corporate-driven
set of policies. This revolutionary way of thinking demands a fundamentally different way of looking at the world and its economy.

For all these reasons (and a few yet to be mentioned), the consumer is
the focus of this book. The consumer is the new primary unit of analysis
in economics and demographics. We will paint a picture of the consumer
in her changing world, but we will focus on the size and age of the population. To put it another way, the short- and long-term changes in population are an essential part of economics and public policy. One way to think
about this change is to consider the behavior of firms and businesses that
have increasingly focused on customer satisfaction in their marketing campaigns. Brand identity focuses on what attracts consumers to products and,
most important, actually motivates them to buy. Businesses have quickly
realized that the consumer is "king," that the consumer's satisfaction and

loyalty is of paramount importance to the survival of their companies. The consumer need not seek the products he wants or needs; rather, the products seek him and his maximal satisfaction. Consumption theory and analysis should become valued as much as production theory in economics. The recent focus of behavioral economics on consumption is an essential and important contribution in the public sphere. There is more work to do in this mostly untapped area of study. We need to examine the utility of different expenditures, the ability to pay for public goods and services, the ability to pay taxes in order to uphold the common good, and the ability to offer possible incentives to enable the purchase of more goods and services. How the consumer responds to these incentives is now central to any serious conversation about the national economy.

The two major transformations of the past century were the Information Revolution and the still-unfolding Global Age. These historical periods clearly influence the structure and behavior of our economy and require, in profound ways, that we develop new tools and a new focus on creating the appropriate public policies to address these fundamental historical transformations. Business is undertaken; even politics and elections think and act in this direction. Now it is time for macroeconomics to start the process of catching up.

The Role of the Consumer in Changing Economic Demographics

One might argue that politics has always explicitly considered demography as an input, through the vehicle of voting and voter satisfaction. Polling and exit analysis along with election strategy examine the electorate and produce extensive demographic analysis of the results. This information used to explain the likely results of future elections. Demographic trends are used extensively in this analysis. The demographic behavior of voters (i.e., how different age groups, different regions, different racial and ethnic groups voted) is a key part of political analysis. Additionally, the growth rates of these demographic groups are the basis of political strategies used in the presidential and other campaigns. There are many front-page press and blog stories during our election cycles that provide full coverage and understanding of how "we the people" influence and affect political decision making. The most recent result of this type of analysis, as identified in the 2016 election cycle, is the political dissatisfaction of the people toward their government and the perceived "establishment." While the depth of the dissatisfaction, expressed by large numbers of individuals in both parties, is unsettling, particularly to the establishment, it is shedding new light on who is in charge—namely, the American people.

Business applies demographic research often to understand the purchasing power of the population. This forms the basis of all market research for products (durable and nondurable). Another important use of demographics is the census, which gathers demographic data for determining the distribution of political representatives and power. When it comes to understanding the economics of the country, demography is an assumption but rarely a primary variable used in analysis. In microeconomics, which studies firms or companies instead of states or nations, consumption functions look at the utility and satisfaction of the consumer toward the product considered. Price is the dynamic variable that finds equilibrium in these studies. When looking at the economics of nations (macroeconomics), "lag variables" measure behavior one or two years prior in order to identify behavioral changes. Introducing changes in the population's behavior does not find its way into the analysis of the economy as a whole. One area that is introducing behavioral analysis is the provision of public goods where the response of the population to incentives and disincentives is considered. When it comes to how changes in the population are directly affecting growth—increases in income, consumption, and payments to government—economists conduct very little analysis. Correcting that deficit is one of the main motivations for the publication of this book.

Long- and Short-Term Demographic Changes

A common explanation for not taking demographics into consideration is that the demographic cycle captures gradual and predictable changes. This was the justification for using lag variables as the primary long-term analytical tool. The exceptions that are truly unpredictable in demographics are war, pestilence, and immigration, which have an enormous effect on all social sciences and institutions one way or another. The predictability of this demographic cycle makes it valuable in policy analysis, and the slow-moving nature of advances in this science demand a new look.

The technological changes that are occurring in medicine, food, transportation, and communication are altering this slow-moving discipline. A recent five-part series in the *Wall Street Journal* by Greg Ip captured the changing nature of our demographics and began exploring its impact on the economy of the United States and the world. Ip starts this series by noting the work of Amlan Roy (at Credit Suisse) who observed that "it took 80 years for the U.S. median age to rise seven years to 30 by 1980 and just 34 more years to climb another eight, to 38. Another example of the rapid change in demographics is the daily repetition of the number of baby boomers who are retiring each day starting in the first decade of this century: 10,000 per day."[4] While this is not the first time a writer has mentioned these numbers, it is one of the earliest examples of an exploration of their economic significance. The most interesting observation of Ip's series is the long-standing fret that the world has too many people. Going forward, Ip notes that the concern will be that it may have too few.

A number of key findings in the 2015 United Nations World Population Forecast support this observation. Fertility rates in 83 countries representing almost half the world's population have declined below replacement levels.[5] Most of Europe, China, and Japan are in this list, while the United States, Brazil, and Russia are included in a low replacement/almost replacement list. In fact, only 3 percent of the world's population lives in countries where the fertility rate is not decreasing, and 21 nations, mainly in Arica, have populations where the fertility rates have a moderate decline. Population in 48 countries will probably decline in the first half of this century.[6] Populations in countries around the world are aging, with the number of people over 80 expected to triple by 2050. While there is a declining population growth rate, the distribution of this decline is probably the single most significant factor affecting the global economy today. For the first time in over half a century, the number of workers worldwide is not growing and will actually decline 5 percent by 2050.[7] This means fewer workers, fewer consumers with higher incomes, and more people aging, all with different consumer demands. The effects of these global changes on the United States are the focus of the chapters that follow.

The Great Depression, the Great Recession, and War

Among the greatest uncertainties in economics is predicting the effect of wars and pestilence on the economy, particularly over the long term. A good way to get a better understanding of how wars and pestilence have affected our economy is to look back at the two most significant military events in our history. These events are the Civil War and World War II. The Civil War resulted in significant losses (including noncombatants) in the population of the country, with the Union and the South combined suffering 750,000 casualties and 281,000 wounded, or 3.28 percent of the total population documented in the 1860 Census (31.4 million people).[8] The immediate and long-term impacts were detrimental to the South and its economic base. The North had a short-term recession, followed by several decades of increased growth. Whether there was a drag on the growth is unknown. Also unknown is the war's impact on the people and the economy over the long term. How many decades of adverse impacts did we experience overall?

The Immigration Act of 1917—best known for imposing a literacy test on some immigrants—had created a "barred zone" expressed in degrees of latitude and longitude, which halted the immigration of most Asians not previously excluded or limited. The first statute to limit most immigration, the Quota Act of 1921, placed numerical limits on European immigration. Looking at the long-term impact, it is interesting to note that a decade before the Great Depression in the 1930s, the Quota Act of 1921 placed limitations on the number of immigrants who could come to the country. We do not have any data on the economic behavior of the nation's population. This capacity started to develop much later in the century; only numerical data are available for this earlier period. What is interesting to note are the demographic limitations and the imposition of the Smoot-Hawley trade barriers prior to the Great Depression. Sound familiar? The time period between the Civil War and the Great Depression, and between World War II and the Great Recession in 2007, is, interestingly, roughly the same—each around 60 years.

The United States suffered over one million casualties in World War II, the largest of any war in our history, but a much smaller percentage of our population (0.075 percent). After the war, a burst of activity followed with the postwar expansion of returning troops and high fertility rates as the baby boomer generation was born. What impact these slow-moving, but highly significant, influences have on growth and economic activity will be examined in the next chapter.

Notes

1. Peter Drucker, "The Rise and Fall of Pluralism," *Wall Street Journal*, June 1, 1999, http://www.wsj.com/articles/SB928182059339889134.

2. Phillip Bobbitt, *Shield of Achilles: War Peace, and the Course of History* (New York: Knopf, 2002), pp. 283–342.

3. Douglass C. North, *Institutions, Institutional Change and Economic Performance* (New York, Cambridge University Press, 1990).

4. Greg Ip, "How Demographics Rule the Global Economy," *Wall Street Journal*, November 22, 2015, http://www.wsj.com/articles/how-demographics-rule-the-global-economy-1448203724.

5. United Nations, Department of Economic and Social Affairs, Population Division, "World Population Prospects: 2015 Revision," 2015, http://www.un.org/en/development/desa/population/events/other/10/index.shtml

6. United Nations, "World Population Prospects," pp. 6–7.

7. Ip, "How Demographics Rule the Global Economy," p. 1.

8. Nese F. De Bruyne and Anne Leland, "American War and Military Operations Casualties: Lists and Statistics," *Congressional Research Services*, January 2, 2015, https://www.fas.org/sgp/crs/natsec/RL32492.pdf.

CHAPTER FOUR

The Demographic Portrait

What Is the Cloud Hanging over the Economy?

Clearly, something is holding the economy back: an unidentified hindrance on our economic growth. There appears to be a drag on growth, not only in the United States, but in other developed and developing countries as well. Our news is filled with stories of the stagflation that has occurred in Japan over the past decade. The Euro Zone's flirting with the same force is cited as a primary reason that we may be heading for our next recession. Even in the developing nations—China, Brazil, and others—slow growth is becoming a problem. We must start by asking what exactly this underlying drag might be. How many articles and pundits have you read and heard that suggest that there is too much debt in the world? Or that fluctuation in the price of oil is causing uncertainty in the global marketplace? Still others suggest that the reserve banks in the world are simply putting too much capital in play, one way or another. The number of possible reasons has reached dizzying heights.

Let's start by looking at the basics. Since the effects are apparently universal, it would be wise for us to begin looking for answers in fundamental factors that are at the core of all economic activity. We will focus on an element that has been missing from the field of economics—namely, a close look at the people who make up the economy and how they are changing. This book will explore the possible root causes of our sluggish economy. I will argue that (1) an increasing aging population earns less income, consumes less, pay less taxes, and requires increased support for pensions and health and (2) the increasing reduction in the number of working-age population who earn more, consumer more and pay more taxes are the twin challenges to economic growth.[1] These are the likely root causes of our economic malaise that will be explored in this book.

For the United States, some might believe I speak only of the baby boomers. Recent reports and press articles in magazines, newspapers, and journals across the country have described how the aging population is going to cause increases in healthcare and pension costs. This is certainly true, but it is also only the tip of the iceberg.

We should not ignore or underestimate the fundamental role of all age groups in the transformation of the economy in the United States, and we should be aware of these same forces globally. We need to ask ourselves: Who are the American people? How are they changing over time? How will these trends affect the economy in the years to come? What are these same forces throughout the world?

How do the dynamics discussed in the previous chapter contribute to our answers of these questions?

Until we shift our perspective and reflect upon these questions, we will be unable to comprehend the past, evaluate our current circumstances, or accurately predict the future. We could find out too late that the light at the end of the tunnel is a train.

The beauty is that we already have at our disposal a lens to see how these questions can be framed and how the economic picture can be brought into focus more clearly through the study of demography. Demography offers a solution precisely because it focuses on people (from the Greek *demos* = population and *graphia* = writing). The objective of this chapter, simply put, is to demonstrate what happens when you closely examine U.S. demographic data and compare them to annual and long-term economic forecasts of the nation. By painting a picture of who we are and how we are changing (in large measure because of the fundamental transformations that were described in the previous chapters), we will gain new insights. You will quickly see that the demographic cycle—that is, the portrayal of us over time—has a substantial effect on incomes, taxes paid, employment, and GDP growth. Enough of an impact, perhaps, that our current inability to quickly escape the Great Recession and return to pre-recession growth rates may be largely a result of it. Furthermore, these impacts are blunting the effectiveness of fiscal and monetary policies that we have relied on in the past to address these challenges. The demographic changes that are occurring are fundamental and enduring, and they transcend economic systems. They are having the same impact on the economic systems in Europe, Asia, and South America.

First, a note on the term "demographic cycle." This is the statistical representation of people over time. Generally, the term refers to who we are, how we age, and what we do as we age. Specifically, the demographic cycle is defined by our vital statistics over time (e.g., gender, age, race, and ethnic composition), population figures, employment and retirement rates, incomes, and expenditures of every variety. The core of demographic inquiry is looking at what happens to us from birth to death. The dynamic elements of this analysis are the factors that influence both ends of this somewhat predictable cycle. The fertility rate of women (i.e., the number of children born to women during their adult lives) is the most important dynamic and is greatly influenced by social, economic, cultural and political influences of the time. At the other end of the life cycle, mortality rates, while altered by these same forces, are also impacted by medical care, health advances, war, and pestilence.

Our primary focus is what is happening at the national level, but there are also differences in the different parts of the country that could also be explored. Changes are occurring between and among cities, states, and regions. Shifting our focus to understanding the demographic cycle and the role that we the people play in the economy will provide new insights. Potential consequences of these demographic changes, possible problems to confront, and policies to consider will be presented. This inquiry of what demographic changes does to the economic system provides a new lens that enables us to explore and develop a new understanding of the puzzling American economy.

Importance of the Individual in the Economy

A big picture enables us to understand the basics, the foundations of economic activity. People are the building blocks of the economy. We have for too long thought of consumption plus investment plus government spending $(C+I+G+(X-M))$ as the building blocks of macroeconomics. In microeconomics, the firm is the building block. But the important thing to consider is that these components are all made up of individuals (who make them work in the short and long term). Take growth of the economy as an example. A dominant two-thirds of general economic growth is determined by growth in the labor force (growth in the number of workers, their skills, and education) and the technology that is altering their productivity. So if our concern is growth in the economy and we do not look at the growth in the working-age population or the potential growth in the number of people who could enter the labor force, our analysis could very well be incorrect. Listening to the policy and political debate of the day, one would think that this is not important. We just need to get more investment through more capital, get government out of the way or have more government intervention, and develop all the new inventions and technologies possible—then we will grow the economy. In fact, increasing our population and growing our working-age population is a challenge that we must confront now at a time when many have a negative view of immigration and many working age populations are simply opting out of the economy. The confusion created by these policy conflicts will be discussed in later chapters.

Another example of public misunderstanding is how government at all levels—federal, state, and local—is funded. Taxes paid by individuals comprise 90 percent of the funds collected. Ten percent is paid by business. The political discourse looks at this 10 percent as the place where solutions to our fiscal problems are to be found. But when you look at the numbers, not enough money can be found there. It follows that the lack of focus on what is happening to individuals, their incomes, and the growth in population—all the primary source of revenues for government—prevents us from coming to a clear understanding and to a real solution. If we want to understand how our economy is working in order to address some of the basic issues of our day, we need to first understand the basic building block of the economy: people, their behavior, and how the composition and makeup of individuals are changing. The insights of the previous chapter on the increasing role of the individual, magnified by global and information transformations, reposition the individual as the key decision maker. Ultimately, it is individual decision making, not firms or the policies of the nation-state, that alters the production cycle. Now we can begin to understand what holds the economy back. This changed focus gives new importance and meaning to looking at individuals and their collective behavior. In our country, we have the tools to analyze these changes and their meaning (to be discussed later in this chapter). We just have to use them in a different way than in the past. Population surveys are not just interesting observations, but they are also the driving force behind a new mode of decision making in our country. This is the basic unit of analysis: individuals who desire new ways of providing for themselves and their families; individuals as wage earners; workers with incomes; consumers and taxpayers with a comprehension of how they are changing. Individuals are not afterthoughts of an imagined construct of how the economy works. They are the drivers and decision makers.

Life Cycle of the Population

Start by thinking of what happened in our own lives. What was our earnings profile as we passed from one phase of life to another? Most likely when we were in our early years, we earned very little income, save part-time work when in school. Our first jobs were more than likely entry-level, low-paying jobs. As we gained experience and pursued opportunities including entrepreneurial initiatives, our incomes started increasing until we reached a peak income. Then our incomes began to decline as we retired (perhaps with some additional income that we picked up) until we reached an age when we stopped working. This has been the life-cycle description of income for decades; from just after the Great Depression through the Great Recession of 2007–2009, there has been ever-increasing growth in the economy with a few recessions. For the most part, there have been increases in income and consumption, and increases in taxes.

So what has changed? The global transformations discussed in the previous chapter will have significant impacts on the way individuals behave as economic actors. There are also changes in the age composition of the population. These forces are now and will continue to change the historic pattern. They will dramatically impact our economic growth by altering our incomes, our consumption, and the amount of taxes we pay.

Baby Boomer Snapshot

To get an understanding of this change, we can look to the *baby boomers,* a generation born between 1946 and 1964 (Table 4.1). Boomers were born to parents looking to rebuild a world that was first confronted with the economic disruption of the Great Depression (which lasted for over a decade), then ravaged by a war that engulfed a large portion of the world. Driven by rebuilding and revitalizing, people returned from war. Marriages and household formations spiked. A new urban form was created with the innovation of the detached single-family home. The ubiquitous automobile gave the freedom to define a new way of living, working, and playing; it also sowed the seeds of the undoing of this new lifestyle. We grew the nation, its cities, and regions in a way that made it affordable and conducive for families to raise children. This resulted in fertility rates spikes to level of 3.7 in the postwar period.[2] This unexpected rapid population increase (almost double the level of the 1920s) was sustained for an entire generation. It created an enormous bulge in population that altered the demographic profile of this country. The impact is still being felt today. Simultaneous with the growth in fertility, a large influx of immigrants started after the war. The postwar economic expansion and the global organizations that were formed contributed to this movement of workers. The war that touched so many nations had the effect of bringing the world closer together. Levels of immigration in the post-1950 era approached levels similar to the early part of the last century. Immigration increased the population and the working-age population, and it also contributed to raising the general fertility rates since the fertility rates were higher than the fertility rate of the domestic born population.

As the boomer generation reached its highest income and tax-paying period, (36–54) in 2001, this cohort (i.e., the group of a 10-year period of a century) was 30 percent of the nation's population, had a 46 percent share of the nation's workers, and earned a majority—54 percent—of the income. They were in the higher-income phase of their earnings life cycle and boosted the nation's income. In the last decade of the twentieth century and the first years of this century, they were the engines of the Clinton economic boom. Not only were they a large generation, but they have also been described as the best-educated labor force in in our history. School districts popped up across the country, and there was an explosion in new colleges and universities. The population of this era had the capacity to change the world.

Their expenditures were 50 percent of the national total, and they collectively paid 57 percent of the taxes paid to all levels of government. Just one decade later (2010), this cohort was just 26 percent of the nation's population but still was 39 percent of the workforce, made 46 percent of the nation's income and 43 percent of the expenditures, and paid a whopping 60 percent all the taxes paid in the country. Even as they entered their twilight in the first decade of the millennium, while they were only 24 percent of the population, they paid 46 percent of the taxes and generated 37 percent of

Table 4.1   Why Do Boomers Matter?

Who Are Baby Boomers (born between 1946– and 1964)			
	As of 2000	As of 2010	As of 2015
Age Ranges	36–54	46–64	51–69
Population Size	89,348,000	81,489,455	75,039,087
Share of Total Population	30%	26%	24%
Number of Employed Workers	53,633,700	51,423,200	44,697,800
Share of Employed Workers	46%	44%	31%
Share of Total Income	54%	46%	37%
Share of Total Expenditures	50%	43%	36%
Share of Taxes Paid	57%	60%	43%

Sources: Population figures are from the Census 2014 American Consumer Survey; workers are from the Bureau of Labor Statistics and Census Population Survey 2015; income, expenditures, and taxes are from the Bureau of Labor Statistics 2014 Consumer Expenditure Survey.

the nation's income. This snapshot of this "too big to fail" generation shows that all population, and all age cohorts in the population, cannot be assumed to be the same when describing the effect of demographics on the economy. Some age cohorts have more workers and fewer older and retired population. Other cohorts have a different profile. The difference in contribution each year and the rapidity of these changes help us understand why population changes could be important. If each cohort's growth is the same over time, there would not be a demographic impact on the economy; but as seen in this snapshot, this was not the case, showing the need to dig deeper into the impact of these changes. Just how important are these changes? What is the significance and size of these changes and will they have a significant impact on the economy?

In reality, some age cohorts have more employed workers than other age cohorts and by a large difference. Similiarly, the total national income generated in some cohorts is significantly larger than others, and there are fewer cohorts of older and retired populations. If each cohort growth were the same over time, these differences would cancel each other out. But this is not what is happening. The differences shown in the large boomer generation cohorts suggest that knowing these differences could be important. Also important is the size and distribution of the successive generations following this "too big to fail" generation. You might ask, "Why did a smaller percentage of the population pay more in taxes and make much more income?" The answer is since consumption makes up two-thirds of the economy and personal related taxes are 90 percent of our government revenues, the changes in the size and composition of cohorts make a big difference. Arguably these changes and their economic consequences sowed the early seeds of the Great Recession and dampened and extended the recovery, and casting a cloud on our future which will be discussed and quantified in later chapters.

The Age Distribution of Populations

The baby boomers began to reach their highest-income years in 2001, just when their incomes began to decline, at age 55. Starting in 2010, they began to retire at a rate of 10,000 workers a day, when changes in the economy began to appear. Incomes in this phase of the boomer income cycle are significantly less, thus a drop in contribution to national income from this part of the population. Boomer participation in the labor force, their incomes, expenditure patterns, and their taxes paid all began to decline, with a major impact on the economy as a whole.

An important question to ask is: Why didn't this generation, the sons and daughters of the greatest generation, continue the growth rate of the population? The cause and reason for the decline in population in following generations can be traced to the demographic dynamic of the decline in the fertility rate. Starting in 1960, the rate dropped from its peak of 3.7 to 1.8 by the turn of the century, a precipitous decline in just one generation. While the fertility rate increased slightly to 2.01 in 2009, the increase was actually the result of immigration and is now falling again. The birthrate of immigrants made up the decline of the fertility rate of those living here, which is actually below replacement rates. This decline in the fertility rate was not just in the United States. The fertility drop occurred throughout the world, even more rapidly in many of the developed countries involved in war, and even in the developing countries. One of the most startling observations about this change is that today only 3 percent of the world's population lives in five countries with a fertility rate that is not decreasing.[3]

What does this mean to our economy?

While the baby boomers grew the economy, they did not produce a progeny that would continue their growth cycle. The result of this change is that in future years there were fewer people in the working-age population. Put simply, there were fewer potential workers. While more workers had previously made higher incomes, consumed more, and paid higher taxes, what followed was, fewer workers, making less income, spending less-with reduced consumption, and less governmental revenue. This is not a complicated set of relationships, but it has gone undiagnosed. The generations following the boomers were smaller and some say not as well educated. For decades, there has been a cry for more money for education and a focus on better education. Robert Putman, in *Kids: The American Dream in Crisis,* suggests that our inability to deal with the demographic implications of inequality is at the heart of this crisis and provides insights on how to correct it.[4]

Notes

1. "Southern California Fiscal Sustainability and Governance Project," Report to the John Randolph Haynes and Dora Haynes Foundation, June 2014.

2. Jonathan V. Last, *What to Expect When No One's Expecting: America's Coming Demographic Disaster* (New York: Encounter Books, 2014), p. 15.

3. "The Astounding Drop in Global Fertility Rates between 1970 and 2014," Brilliant Maps, June 23, 2015, http://brilliantmaps.com/fertility-rates.

4. Robert Putnam, *Kids: The American Dream in Crisis* (New York: Simon & Schuster, 2015).

CHAPTER FIVE

Generation X and the Effects of Population Change

The Paint-by-Numbers Approach to Portraying a Generation

In the last chapter, we learned from the boomers that the age distribution of a nation's population is a key dynamic in economic performance. In addition, our analysis of the boomers provided valuable insight into the hidden benefits (age-dividend) and harms (age-penalty) that can result from population variation between age groups. More data about the population size of the generations that followed the boomers will provide greater clarity about our current situation. As you have probably realized, perceptive economic analysis often comes down to asking the right questions and gathering evidence in the form of quantitative data. In this particular case, we should ask the following questions: What are the population changes in each age cohort over time? How do changes in these populations affect income, expenditures, and taxes paid? Finally, each reader should consider two subquestions since the answers will vary: (1) where are you on the age curve, and (2) how is your contribution affecting the economy?

The problem, in essence, is change over time.

Over the course of our lives, as we age and change, our economic behavior changes, too. As we learned in the last chapter, there is a direct correspondence between age and average annual income. Of course, many of our individual earning and spending habits fall above or below the average of population for any giving year- but, for the cohort on average, the pattern has remained roughly the same for the past 50 years. Take our average income, for example. It initially increases as we age, rapidly over certain decades, almost tripling between the ages of 25 and 45, and continues to rise until its eventual peak at 55. Afterward, our income slowly declines between ages 55 and 65 dropping by more than a fourth over the next decade and by more than a half after age 75 until we stop receiving income altogether. We also know the same is true of expenditures and tax payments.[1] It may seem strange that something as simple as our aging could have such a profound effect on our economy, but if you imagine the process on a national scale, it begins to make more sense. Think of the entire population of the United States, which is estimated at 324 million people in 2016. Now divide the population into different age groups, separated by decade intervals, and then examine the variations in the population size of each generation. Next, apply the percentage change that our age difference has on our income, consumption, and taxes paid. These changes when looked at individually seem miniscule when compared to the size of our economy, but when we calculate them in aggregate on an annual basis and compound them over time, the effects are literally exponential. These changes will be further explained throughout this chapter. As you can imagine, changes like this have a major impact on the economy of a highly populated country like the United States.

Now, a few words about the approach used to create this changing portrait. In the United States Constitution, the census was originally required for the apportionment of representatives. Congress passed separate laws in 1954 when they realized that we needed more data in order to fund a broad range of federal programs. According to the Census Bureau website, from the very first census act, Congress sought "more information than just a headcount."[2] Further, the Department of Commerce enumerates and identifies the vital statistics of the people that comprise our political system and conducts a forecast of the population through three very large surveys that help us understand the size and scope of our economy. First, the American Community Survey (ACS) annually samples over 150,000 people to illustrate changes in individual and labor force behavior in the United States. Second, the Current Population Survey (CPS) annually samples 210,000 individuals who are representative of our country, in order to provide a clear picture of population and employment. Last, the remarkable Consumer Expenditure Survey (CEX) samples in great detail 7,000 households from 91 areas of the United States, collecting 14,000 diaries and five quarterly interviews from each household, reporting how our population spends the money it acquires each year. For the CEX, each consumer unit keeps a diary for two one-week periods, yielding 14,000 diaries a year, and completes an interview once per quarter for five consecutive quarters.

The CEX collects data from each consumer on an ongoing basis in 91 diverse areas of the United States.

Since individuals determine the majority of all economic activity, these remarkable surveys enable us to understand how the machinery of our economy works. The collective influence of individual behavior determines most of the historically important issues at the center of our national dialogue. We can use these surveys to evaluate the likely effects of demographic shifts in our population, such as age, consumer expenditures, employment, gender, income, nationality, number of people, and socioeconomic status.

One of the most significant changes studied by the CEX is labor force participation—that is, changes in who is working, is looking for work, or has dropped out of the labor force completely. Another useful subject covered in this survey is total consumer income and expenditures, which includes details regarding the source of income and the way the income is spent. The CEX provides such impressively robust detail that we could apply the same method to study any particular category of consumer expenditures we were interested in, including goods, services, health, education, or gifts. These surveys provide the big-data capacity to look at our economy in ways not possible in the past. Our task is to now ask the right questions and construct the methods that will answer them.

Changing Population in Age Cohorts

Why was Generation X, born 1964–1980, the generation behind the boomers, a smaller population? The economy during the period of their birth was resilient; and, in spite of several recessionary periods, national growth was still positive, with GDP growth above 3.5 percent for decades. A significant change in our economic base occurred during this period. The Cold War concluded and a major decline in defense spending followed as a result, but at the same time, the advent of information technology added a new and exciting dimension to our economy. Therefore, economic reasons were probably not the cause. The demographic driver was a decline in the fertility rate due to factors including the evolving role of women and changes in family structure and household formation. Pharmaceutical technology enabled couples to limit the number of children with the advent of the Pill and other advances in contraception, while laws protected a woman's right to choose (*Roe v. Wade*). Add to this public policies, including land use and development decisions that made raising children difficult and expensive, and you have a profound change in cultural and social priorities whose result is a substantial decline in the fertility rate. Jonathan V.

Last characterized this social metamorphosis in a work entitled *What to Expect When No One's Expecting*.[3]

All these changes have resulted in generations that are smaller in absolute numbers. The generation following the baby boomers, Generation X, had 20 million fewer people. The next generation, the Millennials (1981–1998), had 10 million fewer people than Gen X. The declining fertility rate, of course, led to a smaller population in certain age groups that is hard to recognize because many baby boomers are only starting to reach the last stages of their lives. The other demographic driver, immigration, has more uncertainty attached to it, primarily for political reasons. The deceleration of economic and labor growth over the past 15 years has led voters to view immigrants, willing to work at lower wages, as taking jobs from them. This divisive issue has created a political stalemate in Congress, preventing reform in national policies on immigration. This is particularly true of current policy regarding the 11.3 million unauthorized immigrants in the country, many of whom have children born in the United States. The 2014 Census forecast, which is used as a baseline in this book, is lower than previous estimates of immigration because of input from local surveys and information from countries that are the source of migrants. These factors led the Census Bureau to lower its 2012 forecast of immigration from 65.6 million to 41.2 million people coming to the United States by 2060.[4] In just two years, the forecast was reduced by almost 38 percent. The 2016 presidential election cycle and the election of Donald Trump call even this number into question given the current outrage against immigrants in the country. The demographic and economic analysis of this book suggests that on economic grounds this policy is misguided. The changing dynamics of the global economy and the substantial decline in the fertility rate make clear: if we continue the current trend, the population of the United States, particularly the working-age population, will not be large enough to maintain a thriving economy.

The final factor to consider, and the one most responsible for the continuing population size of the baby boomers, is life expectancy. As a nation, our priorities are to improve health, well-being, and extend our lives. The newest forecasts suggest that life expectancy should reach the mid-80s by the middle of the 21st century, with women still expected to live longer than men, though the life expectancy gap is shrinking. By 2035, some forecasters project that the population aged 65 and older will reach 78 million in the United States, which is more than a 50 percent increase from the 46 million of today. When you compare this number to the other contributing factors, it is reasonable to conclude that the primary driver of population growth is increasing life expectancy. People over 65 will soon be a larger group than those below the age of 18.

Incidentally, when you combine the number of people under 18 with those over the age of 65, the sum defines the number of people typically categorized as in the dependent age group. When you take this number and divide it by the number of people in the working-age population, you come up with the dependency ratio (the ratio of workers to dependent-age population). Although the improvement in life expectancy is a cause for celebration in so far as it represents a significant improvement in the quality of our lives, it does have a serious impact on the economy. Consequently, we need to reevaluate U.S. economic policy resulting from this changing age of our population, a concept that we will discuss later in the book.

Age Forecast of the Nation

What is the forecasted population for the country? What is the expected population of each age group in the decades to come? What are the economic and political implications of these numbers? Which public policy plans are in place to adapt to these changing numbers and prepare for the future? From the discussion of changes in income over the life cycle and the changes in age-cohort distribution, we can only conclude that these are the questions we need to answer in order to plan the nation's future. With our short-term focus as a society, we live as existential beings in the here and now, generally only thinking about how to get through the day, the week, or the month, depending on socioeconomic status. A longer-term focus for us is planning our next holiday or vacation. Our business leaders think about the next quarter, and our political leaders think about the next election. Since our focus is on building the best bridge to the future, it would be wise to think about the world that our children will inherit or, even more appropriately, the world our grandchildren will inherit.

Generally, we consider these long-term plans as irrelevant because predictions are more likely to be wrong. Short of war and catastrophes, there is a high degree of predictability in the science of demography, however, because the demographic cycle appears to follow a stable pattern. After all, one thing we are sure of is that we have a beginning and end to our lives. Predicting the population patterns of a nation by applying fertility rates, life expectancy, and immigration rates tend to yield forecasts that are close to the actual numbers. Since this life cycle will have significant economic impacts, a closer examination could provide insights into the shape of our economic future. The census process, the official enumeration of our nation, is a starting point for this examination. The most recent forecast used lowered immigration rates and combined them with the births and deaths added by the succession of generations of natural-born citizens. These numbers predicted the future population and an estimate the working-age population for age cohorts in the United States. It is a picture of the age distribution of the population over time, displaying age groups of the past as they move into the future. There are multiple views on the differences surrounding the assumptions of this forecast, as one might imagine, but it provides a starting point for forecasting the future.

Not only is the population in the nation changing, but households are also changing in both composition and age. "Household" is usually defined as a grouping of people who share a place to live and eat together, and the household is the best unit of measurement to explain expenditure patterns. As the family structure is changing, it follows that there is a change in the household composition. As we marry later (or even defer marriage altogether) and our divorce rate increases, more single-member households are formed. The decline in the fertility rate in both the resident population and immigrant population typically results in fewer children per household. More single-parent families and more single-gender households are forming than ever before. Baby boomers will age and die, contributing to a large increase in single households.

Think of the expenditure changes that this rapidly changing household pattern will produce. The increase in single parents with fewer children means there will be fewer purchases from each household. In addition, demographic economics has found as a general rule that the older the household, the smaller the expenditures. Expenditure patterns in the modern household are significantly lower than in the past. In addition, we can expect major changes in the types of products we consume as well as the amount of them. Smaller housing units will become the norm. Furthermore, older households are significantly different from newer households, especially those with young children, whose largest purchases generally include homes, furniture, and medical and education expenses for children. Yet heads of households 65 years and older are projected to account for almost all of the household growth between 2010 and 2020, and over three-quarters of the growth (77 percent) for 2020–2035.[5] So, in addition to looking at the income cycle, we also need to take into account the changing household formations to understand the transformation of the expenditure cycle that is underway.

We will use tables and charts as evidence in our paint-by-numbers approach. Table 5.1 is a presentation of the Department of Commerce forecast of population, distributed according to the age categories used to

Table 5.1 U.S. Population Changes, 1980–2035

Historical and Projected U.S. Population Changes (Growth) by Age Cohorts

	1980–1990	1990–2000	2000–2010	2010–2015	2015–2020	2020–2035
15–24	(5,712,501)	2,409,564	4,442,451	205,954	(725,419)	781,440
25–34	6,094,093	(3,284,208)	1,172,224	3,068,552	2,757,436	555,616
35–44	11,944,193	7,569,624	(4,077,921)	(546,181)	2,103,345	6,907,639
45–54	2,423,299	12,454,866	7,328,764	(1,878,519)	(2,286,261)	5,334,543
55–64	(554,952)	3,126,761	12,208,045	4,421,136	2,115,500	3,407,795)
65–74	2,525,953	284,428	3,322,443	5,880,652	5,481,093	5,086,868
75+	3,166,451	3,465,494	1,953,788	1,681,609	3,129,689	17,704,986
Total	19,886,536	26,026,529	26,349,794	12,833,203	12,575,383	32,963,297

Sources: 1970–2010, U.S. Decennial Census; 2014–2060, 2014 National Population Projections, U.S. Census Bureau.

create our income life cycle. Essentially, Table 5.1 is a summary of this forecast by decade of the working-age population from 1980 up to 2035. The number in each row in the table is the change in the population in the decade from the previous decade. For example there was a 5,712,501-person increase in population in the number of 15 to 24 year population for the 1980–1990 decade. The total number of working age and elderly population in the 1980–1990 decade is 19,886,536.

As you can see, the population as a whole is growing, but those who contribute financially in income, consumption, and taxes paid are either declining or growing at a much slower rate than those who do not contribute. With fewer people in the age cohorts between 25 and 65 (the primary range of the working-age population) relative to the older population cohorts 65 and above, there will likely be a negative effect on the economy and government revenues for a very long time. For example there were over 4 million fewer 35–44 higher pay working age population in the decade of the great recession. Extend this into the decade we are now in. There were almost 1.9 million fewer higher earning working age population in the first five years of this decade and 2.3 million people in the last part of our current decade. The question is not: is there a negative impact, but rather how large is the negative impact.

This change in the working age population could have such a fundamental effect on the economy that I developed a separate illustration, Figure 5.1,

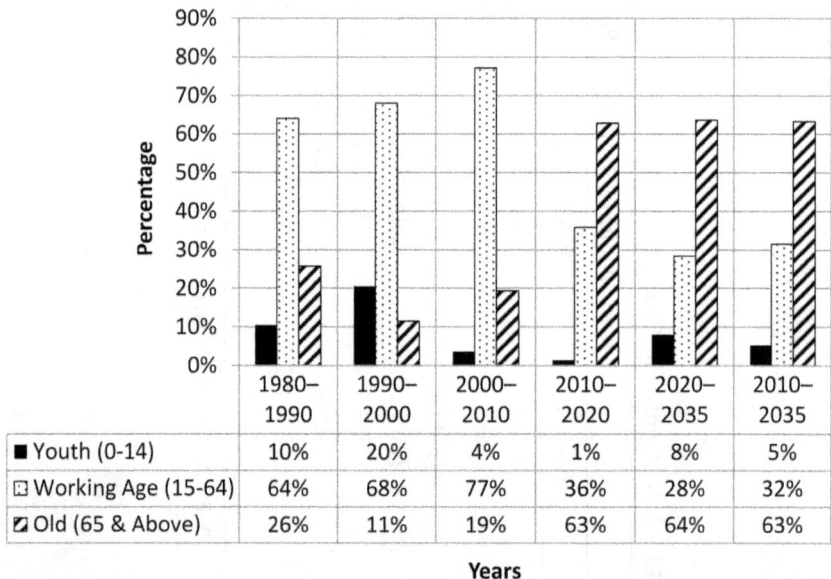

	1980–1990	1990–2000	2000–2010	2010–2020	2020–2035	2010–2035
■ Youth (0-14)	10%	20%	4%	1%	8%	5%
▣ Working Age (15-64)	64%	68%	77%	36%	28%	32%
◪ Old (65 & Above)	26%	11%	19%	63%	64%	63%

Years

Figure 5.1   U.S. Population Growth by Age Cohort 1980-2035

Source: U.S. Census, Population Projections, 2014.

in order to show the growth rate in the number of the young, working-age population and those who are of retirement age. This figure shows an increase in the working-age population throughout the 1980s well into the first decade of the millennium, with growth rates as high as 77 percent. Then almost like falling off a cliff, it drops in the current decade, with growth rates in the low 30 percent range, and it never recovers. The decline of the aging population prior to the turn of the 21st century (19.6 percent) was equally as dramatic as its rapid rise ever since. Demographers predict that over half of the total population increases in the future will be due to increases in the elderly population, which is living longer. These numbers will be presented on charts so that you can begin visualizing the transformation that will occur and better understand the magnitude of this effect on the economy.

Changes in Income and Expenditures over Time

Our next step is to take the changes in earning and spending habits that occur over the life cycle, apply this formula to the different populations of each age group, and calculate the expected changes in income, expenditures (consumption), and taxes paid. This is the paint-by-numbers approach to creating the portrait of a generation. The first step of this approach is to determine the actual change in the population per age group in the past and then project this change into the future. The Consumer Expenditure Survey (CEX) provides a glimpse of the larger picture of employment in our nation by accounting for three major categories: employment, income, and expenditures. First, the CEX tells us who is available to work, who is employed, and which sector employs them—private, government, or nonprofit. Second, it provides a detailed account of how much money Americans are earning on average as well as which source they are receiving it from: employment, investments, or government transfer payments (e.g., welfare). Finally, this survey tells us how the average American spends his or her income: consumption of goods and services (and even whether domestic or foreign in origin), charitable contributions, and tax payments at all levels of government. Since the CEX survey contains the age of the subjects of their study, we can categorize the income, expenditures, and tax payments according to each age group, as we have done in the tables below.

Figure 5.2 uses data from the CEX of 2010, which is the same year that the Census Bureau conducted the census for the entire country. Subsequent CEX surveys, of income, expenditures, and taxes paid per household, are consistent with this table in terms of dollars in each age category. The main difference between them is that Table 5.1 divides the people into

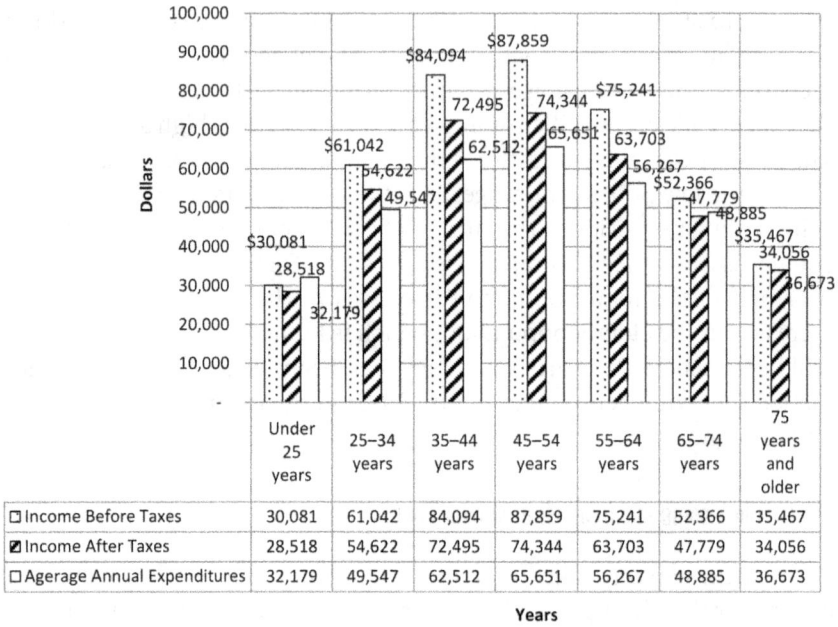

	Under 25 years	25–34 years	35–44 years	45–54 years	55–64 years	65–74 years	75 years and older
☐ Income Before Taxes	30,081	61,042	84,094	87,859	75,241	52,366	35,467
▨ Income After Taxes	28,518	54,622	72,495	74,344	63,703	47,779	34,056
☐ Agerage Annual Expenditures	32,179	49,547	62,512	65,651	56,267	48,885	36,673

Years

Figure 5.2   Income and Expenditure per Household Distributed by Age
Source: Consumer Expenditure Survey, 2014.

three main categories—young, working age, and old—and then focuses on
the fluctuation of population size over five decades. Figure 5.2, on the other
hand, focuses strictly on 2010, divides the population into multiple age
groups (on the horizontal axis), and then measures their financial contributions by dollar amount on the vertical axis. Within each age cohort, we can
see the amount of dollars proportioned to income, expenditures, and taxes
paid in 2010. More recent CEX information shows the same distributions.
The 2010 data was used since the national census was conducted this year.

"Income" includes all wages, tips, gifts, earnings from investment, as well
as all government transfer payments—Social Security, food stamps, general relief, and welfare for families with dependents. The greatest increases
occur between ages 25 and 45, when income almost triples. In this period,
we generally make career decisions that move from entry-level jobs to better employment opportunities that take advantage of our increasing experience and professional development. Consequently, we typically achieve
our highest income level between 45 and 55 years old. Figure 5.2 shows
that in the next decade, our income starts declining, 14 percent between 55
through 65 years—falling over $11,000 per household, each year. Over the
next decade, our income declines by 28 percent, descending over $18,000

per year, each year; after 75 years, it declines over 57 percent, over $18,000 per household. Since there are so many more increases in population in the older age cohorts than in the younger cohorts, these decreases in income begin to add up to substantial numbers. Moreover, the rate of increase in the income cycle is steeper than the rate of decline, which further highlights the importance of increasing our working-age population.

Expenditures follow a similar trajectory and include all consumption, entertainment, recreation, vacations, acquiring capital assets, and investments. Savings is included in the difference between expenditures and after-tax income. The period of greatest savings is in the growth periods of our income cycle as individuals, through various vehicles, save for their later years. The table also includes a calculation of the average income before and after taxes, and average expenditures for each cohort.

The Effect of These Changes on Government

Since personal taxes constitute 90 percent of all revenues paid to governments at all levels—federal, state, and local—the impact of these demographic changes is both interesting and important to the operation of government. Taxes paid include 17 different tax brackets that are paid to all levels of government and include income taxes, fees for government services, property and vehicle taxes, tolls, the tobacco tax, capital gains, and other tax areas. Like income and expenditures, individuals express taxes as annual payments. Tax credits that are allowed by state and local governments and transfer back to individuals are also included. The negative number in the under-25 years reflects this. The continual payment of taxes in the over-75 cohort shows a higher amount of property taxes reflecting the ongoing nature of local property taxes for individuals who continue to live in homes.

In Figure 5.3, the vertical axis is the dollar amount per household (paid in taxes), and the horizontal axis is cohort years. Within each cohort are the income taxes paid to federal and state governments, and all other taxes (which includes property taxes). At the state and local levels, all general and special districts are included. The slope of the increases and decreases in the federal and state taxes columns is much steeper than the income and expenditures changes, which is in part due to the taxes' progressive nature. Changes among cohorts can be several hundred percent in both directions between the decades. Also, the decline in the taxes-paid columns is almost as steep as the increases in the tax columns, which signals that the negative result of demographic impact on taxes paid to government will be much more severe.

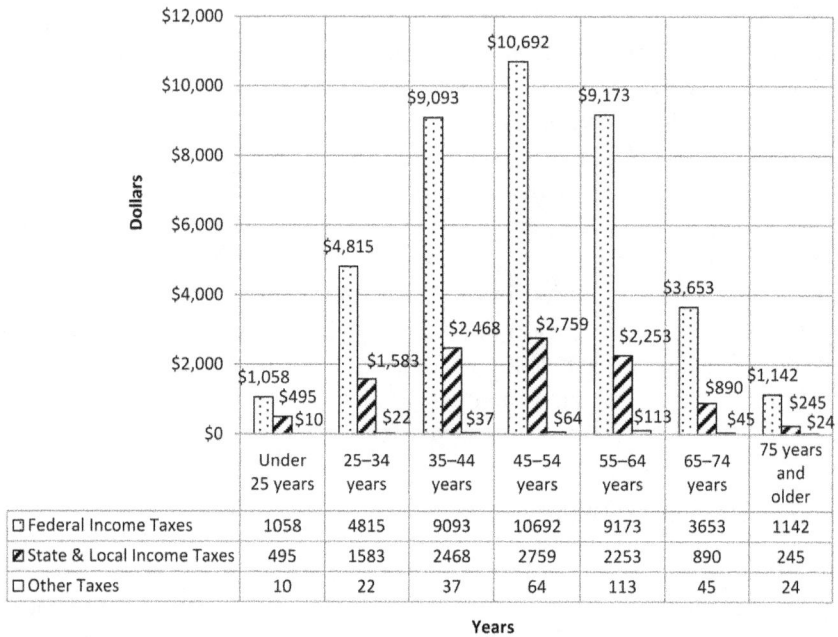

	Under 25 years	25–34 years	35–44 years	45–54 years	55–64 years	65–74 years	75 years and older
☐ Federal Income Taxes	1058	4815	9093	10692	9173	3653	1142
▨ State & Local Income Taxes	495	1583	2468	2759	2253	890	245
☐ Other Taxes	10	22	37	64	113	45	24

Years

Figure 5.3   Changes in Taxes Paid Distributed by Age (Dollars per Household)
Source: Consumer Expenditure Survey 2014, BLS.

These tables represent how individuals on average make these decisions. It also shows that incomes, expenditures, and taxes paid rise and then decline as we age. As you might recall, Table 5.1 demonstrates that the growth in the number of older people is larger than the growth of working-age people, which signals that these demographic impacts on income, expenditures, and taxes paid are negative and, given the size of these changes, could be significant. Finally, if household formations are primarily over 55, then nationally this pattern could have further negative effects on expenditures. Since these changes per household each year in the over-55 columns are large, ranging from $11,000 to $18,000, these impacts are significant and will be discussed in later chapters.

Painting generational changes over time by combining Baby Boomers, Generation X and finally Millenials gives us a portrait of the effect that aging has on the distribution of population with the United States. This is the picture of who we are and how many people exist in each year by their age. Our use of the big data set of Consumer Expenditure enables us to capture the economic behavior of this population distribution. The picture we create appears to have problematic economic implications. To summarize, there is a substantial increase in the number of older people., While they are able to enjoy a longer life with many rewards such as spending time enjoying the fruits of their labor and watching their grandchildren grow, they have less income; they spend less than they did when they were working; and collectively they pay less taxes. How to interpret this portrait and understand the implications of this transformational demographic is described in later chapters.

Notes

1. *America 2050*, "Demography Is Economic Destiny," http://www.america2050 .org/Pisano-Demography.pdf.

2. U.S. Census, "Frequently Asked Questions," June 7, 2016, https://ask.cenus .gov.

3. Jonathan V. Last, *What to Expect When No One Is Expecting: America's Coming Demographic Disaster* (New York: Encounter Books, 2014), p. 15.

4. U.S. Census Department, "What a Difference Four Years Make: U.S. Population Projected to Grow at a Slower Pace over the Next Five Decades," December 12, 2016, http://blogs.census.gov/2012/12/12/what-a-difference-four-years -make-u-s-population-projected-to-grow-at-a-slower-pace-over-the-next-five -decades.

5. This information is from the data background for Figure 5.2.

CHAPTER SIX

What This Portrait Tells Us

Lessons Learned: Painting by Numbers

In the last chapter, we created a portrait of the U.S. economy, using the "paint by numbers" approach, that revealed the actual economic consequences of demographic changes. The picture is not positive. It appears to conflict with the results of the recent 2016 presidential election—namely, the voters' conclusion that we have too many people, particularly too may immigrants, and we do not have sufficient opportunities for our existing population. This contradiction is a large part of the economic puzzle in our American economy today. What can we learn from the economic-based demographic portrait of America that can enable us to understand this apparent conflict?

To understand the past economic and political impacts of these changes and predict future repercussions, we need to look at a national population forecast. We will start with the population forecast of the 2014 Census, which is very close to current conditions. This will allow us to unravel the tangled roots of the current economic and political maze. The next point of analysis will be a projection to 2020, the next election cycle. This will give us a solid vantage point to preview the policy implications and political debates we can expect in the United States in the future. Finally, we will examine projections to 2035 that will allow us to predict the probable longer-term future for our children and grandchildren and get a glimpse of our legacy. How will our country deal with the demographic permutations in the future? Future changes will be even more profound as the current transformations we are experiencing.

As we saw in the previous chapter, the overall population changes have been increasing on a global scale. The United States is able to avoid the economic stagflation in Japan and Western Europe caused by population decline. Many of our economic policies are dependent on population growth, which is good news, and the US has more policy options than other developed countries.

The troubling news, however, is that the native-born citizens who will live in the United States during the period 2014 to 2035 will only be responsible for 22 percent of the population growth because of the drop in the fertility rate of women. On the other hand, immigrants, the foreign-born population, are projected to have a 78 percent increase.[1] If the current behavior continues, in fact, most of our increases in population will come either from people living longer or from births of immigrant children. What is surprising is that these percentages were predicated on a substantial reduction in immigration coming into the United States—a 38 percent decrease in the 2014 forecast from the Census 2008 forecast. The reduction by Census was based on survey data from other countries. Since the fertility rate of women is declining globally, even in developing countries, the rate of the world's population growth is decreasing. Remember, only 3 percent of world population resides in countries where the fertility rate is increasing. Recent drops in immigration rates as the result of an upsurge in anti-immigration laws, increases in border patrol, and a rising number of deportations of undocumented immigrants should concern us since these measures will dampen population growth and, by extension, economic growth. (Two-thirds of economic growth in recent economic history is the result of growth of our working-age population.) The discord in the political campaign and our inability over the past decade to agree on an immigration framework cast a cloud over our overall growth policy. If we are not able to address the short-term issues causing this political impasse, and we further reduce immigration, then the economic consequences of the demographic impact could be much larger and much more detrimental than those described in this book.

The most problematic data is the reduction of the working-age population. Today, this age group is 62 percent of the nation's population, and it will reduce by over 3.1 million people (or 1 percent of the population) in just six years. By 2035, the working-age population will be 5 percent smaller, over 19 million people, and this includes immigrants. In a complete picture of the age cycle, the percentage of the total population over 65 is growing by over 35 million people. We have almost twice the growth in the aging/retiring population than in the working population. Given the number of boomers who are retiring at a rate of 10,000 per day, by 2020 over 3.6 million people will have retired. So if we look at the income, consumption, and tax-age columns and take into account that the income of workers is much higher than that of retirees, it makes perfect sense why median per capita incomes, when adjusted for inflation, are not growing. It is no wonder that

Americans have not received a wage increase since the turn of the millennium and that we observe increases in income inequity. We can see that in the snapshot of the boomers,the change began at the turn of the millennium. It was most likely a major contributing factor to the Great Recession and a precursor to the current hand wringing over the failure of incomes to rise. When we look at the breakdown of age in the tax-paying columns, we can see how the aging of the population contributes to the reduction in taxes paid to all levels of government. These changes in the working-age population and in retirees show how significant these impacts in income and tax-payment reductions are—so much so that they are creating fiscal pressure for governments at all levels. What is clear is that the natural increases and decreases in income that occur over the aging cycle, coupled with the changes in the number of people in each age cohort, are having a huge effect. These impacts are further explained and quantified in later chapters.

How Do We Quantify These Impacts?

We can measure just how large the impact is by using two of the surveys with which we have become familiar. The databases of the Census Forecast and the CEX surveys were used for our portrait. The model sums the income, consumption, and taxes-paid changes and applies that sum to all the changes in the age cohorts over time. Basically, the steps are to take the age, income, expenditure, and taxes-paid curves and convert them into percentage changes per year for each variable's elasticity.[2] This tells us how each variable responds to time.

This approach is similar to the long-standing practice of determining how sensitive a product is to changing prices or the price elasticity of demand. As prices rise, businesses sell fewer products. The reverse is true when prices fall. Instead of product to price sensitivity, we calculate the sensitivity that income has to changes over time. As we increase in age, our incomes rise at first but eventually begin to decline, which we will call the "age elasticity of income." Now if we apply this elasticity to the age-population forecast and the changes in the population in each age cohort, the result is an age-adjusted forecast of income, expenditures, and taxes paid. Next, we compare this to a baseline forecast with no age adjustment and, finally, compare the two forecasts. Baselines are a norm used in the practice of forecasting that assumes a condition where nothing changes and compares this condition to changes in policies in order to predict future economic outcomes.

It is worth noting that this analysis takes forecasting a step further by looking at the assumptions that go into our economic calculations. It also examines what happens to our economic analysis of growth and our fiscal and monetary policies when we consider the dynamic effect of this input assumption. Business-cycle implications and policy changes that affect the "ups and downs" of the economy are not an explicit part of this analysis; however, as explained earlier, we can test these cyclical changes, too, through sensitivity analysis. Similarly, the reason for analyzing multiple forecasts is to gather enough data from which to depict how the individual members of our total national population behave under different time periods, policies, and conditions. It also allows us to consider, collectively by age group, behavior over time as individuals go through their own aging cycle.

The CEX surveys were conducted annually, starting in 1984. Prior to this time, we did not have the usefulness of income and expenditure data per individuals. You might say this year introduced the era of big data in economics. Using multiple (CEX) surveys enables understanding how individuals make decisions with different public policies and under different economic periods and conditions. In several of the years, the country was in recession: 1990 and 2000. In other years, there was the passage of the Reagan and Bush tax cuts and the enactment of the Great Recession recovery measures, in terms of both fiscal and monetary policies. To capture the changes in individual behavior, multiple-model-run surveys were conducted for 1984, 1990, 2000, 2005, 2009, 2010, 2011, and 2014 (the last published survey available). Additional analyses using income and tax data from Internal Revenue Service (IRS) files assessed whether the CEX surveys were collecting data such as income from higher-income wage earners correctly. The CEX surveys were determined usable because the differences were not significant. Comparing the results of the multiyear runs shows consistency in the behavior of individuals in their income, consumption/ expenditures, and taxes paid. This result enables us to assess the influence that fluctuating demography has on the economy and the revenues paid to government. These results are depicted graphically and numerically in Figure 6.1. This figure also shows that changes in demography have a very large impact, sometimes greater than fiscal and monetary measures, all of which will be explained in later chapters.

The most recent databases, the 2014 Census Forecast and 2014 CEX, were used to tell our story of how demographic changes affect the economy. The result of the model's conclusion, mapped in Figure 6.1, is presented for income, expenditures, and taxes paid from 1980 to 2035. Looking back over 30 years enables us to see past tendencies, test policy, and historical behavior. Looking forward provides a prophetic window into the sequence between now and the next presidential campaign of 2020. It will also provide us with the opportunity to evaluate the current policy rhetoric and confusing economic explanations. The use of 2035 forecasts the world our children and grandchildren will inherit.

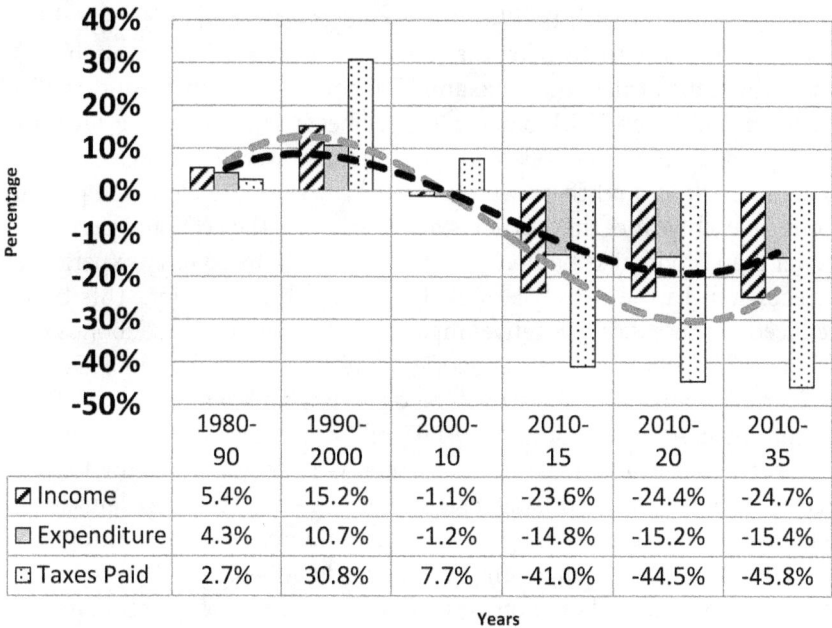

	1980-90	1990-2000	2000-10	2010-15	2010-20	2010-35
▨ Income	5.4%	15.2%	-1.1%	-23.6%	-24.4%	-24.7%
☐ Expenditure	4.3%	10.7%	-1.2%	-14.8%	-15.2%	-15.4%
⊡ Taxes Paid	2.7%	30.8%	7.7%	-41.0%	-44.5%	-45.8%

Years

Figure 6.1   Demographic Bonus and Penalties, 1980–2035 (Percentage Change in Growth and Decline)

Source: Consumer Expenditure Survey 2014.

The vertical axis of the figure delineates the positive and negative impacts of demographic changes. The positive impacts on the economy occur when the working-age population is larger and, thus incomes, expenditures, and taxes paid increase while fewer people retire and there are less income, expenditures, and taxes-paid decreases. The negative percentages simply capture the reverse: working-age populations are growing slower—relatively fewer make more income expenditures and pay more taxes, and many more retirees are making less income, consuming less and paying less taxes. The horizontal axis shows different time periods so that the impacts are evaluated during the different time periods. The past decades provide an opportunity to look at periods with the higher labor-force growth years of the boomers and lower growth in the aging population. The reverse is happening in the future. The analysis for all eight simulations with all their different policy and economic differences demonstrates that using different (CEX) surveys generated consistent results.

Figure 6.1 demonstrates that between 1980 and 2000, before the peaking of the baby boomers' income and its decline during retirement age, is what we call an "age dividend." Expansion of the working-age population with gains in income, expenditures, and taxes paid made a positive contribution to growth in all of these categories. The percentage differences of the growth rate for the age cohorts from 1980 through 2035 show the transformation. For example, income growth percentages 1990 through 2000 were 15.1 percent higher because of the more favorable demographics of the period. The baby boomers were reaching maximum income markets, and there were fewer boomers in the older age populations. In each year of that decade starting in 1990, the economy performed better than economists had projected even though the country experienced a recession. In the early years of the 1990–1991 recession, this bonus reduced the recession's negative impact. In the later years, this bonus contributed $22.5 billion to the economy in 1989, $57.7 billion in 1990, and $102.8 billion in 1991. The size of the demographic bonuses was a $182.95 billion increase in GDP and a $141.43 billion increase in income, had an immediate positive increase on the economy-no delays or waiting for projects to be built. The surprising insight from the size of the age bonus is that when you sum income changes of the large number of people involved in these demographic changes the results are large—bigger than we might imagine. The size of these bonuses, given that the size of the economy was $10.3 trillion (30% smaller than the economy of the Great Recession), was a significant contribution to the performance of economy. This bonus was an annual catalyst to growth, and at a compounding rate, in each year of the decade.

It is important to note that the increases identified here are solely the result of changes in our population age structure. Simply stated, demographic changes in the population, and the economic behavior that naturally follows these changes were the source of surprising and fortuitous gains. This contributed to higher GDP growth, higher consumption, and increased payments to the treasuries of all governmental agencies. Another way of explaining the "demographic age dividend" is that the ever-increasing working-age population meant more individuals with growing incomes, who spent more money on goods and services and paid an ever-increasing amount of taxes. At the same time, there was not significant growth in the aging population, who made less, consumed less, and paid less taxes. The economic forecasts of the time missed this finer-grained analysis generated by demographic changes. As a result, they attributed the economic growth to fiscal and monetary policies alone. Today, two decades later, our forecasts still do not take into consideration the changing age and other demographic characteristics that are so important in developing the right public policies and strategies for economic growth.

Since the baby boom era, policies for growth, for provision of services, for calculating pensions, retirement, and health benefits adjustments, and for budgeting at all levels of government have reflected the results of this "demographic age dividend." Policies are all level of government were codified based on the economic performance of this time. Unfortunately, these embedded policies continue into the future, even though the bonus is not continuing. In fact, as seen in Figure 6.1, it turned into a penalty at the turn of the century, but the adopted policies continue. In part this is the reason we have the governmental fiscal mess that we have today. For example, the "demographic taxes-paid bonus" to all levels of government, for the 1989–1991 period (discussed earlier), was up to $36.5 billion, $67.2 billion, and $85.2 billion in constant 2015 dollars.

After this period, starting around 2001, the demographic transformation changed from positive to negative. The era of the "demographic age penalty," the era we are in now, began and the size of the penalties are several times larger than the bonuses, discussed in future chapters. In this era, there is smaller growth in income, expenditures, and taxes paid. This penalty has the inverse effect on the economy as the age dividend. Unfortunately, it kicked in during the first decade of the millennium just as the Internet bubble burst. While a brief boom in the housing market occurred, it was followed by severe overleveraging that caused the bubble to burst and the Great Recession to begin. One must wonder what was the effect of the unrecognized demographic age dividend on policy makers? Did we unknowingly contribute to the bubble? The answer is yes. It also created a bubble effect on economic performance in the decade generating a false sense of economic performance that could not be sustained once the demographic cycle turned as it did to a penalty. The main conclusion from the analysis of the data is that demography makes a difference in the performance of all three variables (income, consumption, and taxes paid). The model was able to quantify this behavior.

At the turn of the millennium, the percentages in this chart can be interpreted in a similar fashion, except that the bonus changes as the boomers start to reach their maximum-earning years and begin to retire, mid-decade. Gen X, the generation that follows, has an even smaller working-age population. The year 2000 ushered in a new century, and along with it a demographic transformation quietly commenced. It will continue to play out for at least a half-century. If the fertility rate of women continues to decline, and immigration continues to slow, this demographic convergence may continue. Collective individual choices or democratically conceived collective choice will impact our economy with consequences for the operation of our government. These changes are creating both political and economic uncertainty. Demographic changes are the unrecognized driving force behind the changes in our entire political dynamic.

Emergence of the Demographic Age Penalty

The size of the "demographic penalty" for income, expenditures, and taxes paid affects changes in our incomes, expenditures, and the amount of taxes that we as individuals pay to our government. The GDP in 2011 was $16.2 trillion, and a GDP penalty of 24.6 percent (or $472 billion) was not added to the GDP. Just as a bonus is a hidden addition to the economy creating a bubble effect, a penalty is its opposite, a hidden or unrealized amount of income not realized in our national income accounts that can be measured. The United States currently has a population with fewer people in the working-age category, and, in addition, this population is growing at a slower rate. At the same time, there are increasing numbers in the aging population set to retire. When you combine the income effects of fewer workers and more elderly, who are not contributing to the national income, you can identify a demographic penalty—an unrealized amount of income that will not be added to our economy. The GDP penalty for 2016 was $646 billion that was not added to the $18.6 trillion economy due to these demographic changes. This was almost twice the size of the 2 percent real growth in the economy last year. Considering the compounding effect of growth, the average penalty between now and 2035 will be $1.4 trillion per year in constant 2015 dollars and will have a significant effect on the economy (which we will examine in the next chapter).

The taxes paid by individuals, who pay 90 percent of all taxes paid to all levels of the government, are impacted even more. The steeper reductions in taxes paid as we age causes the penalty in percentages to be greater than its effect on income or expenditures. The taxes-paid penalty grows from positive 7.7 percent increase in the growth of taxes paid at the turn of the century to negative 45.8 percent annual reduction in the growth of taxes paid each year in the current decade. The bonus was positive in 2001 and turned negative at the end of the decade to reach a sizeable penalty of $250.3 billion of unrealized taxes in 2015, and it will reach $857 billion in constant 2015 dollars per year in 2035. The penalty is of such sufficient size that it raises questions about the fiscal viability of government at every level. Already there is a political debate over the fiscal condition of government, with Democrats advocating more revenues or tax increases and Republicans recommending a reduction or right-sizing of government. As these penalties continue, further reductions will occur in future revenues, which will only intensify the debate.

There are dramatic consequences if the age structure of the population does not change. We need to further understand these age-structure changes. We need to know what is causing them and make these demographic concepts part of our policy and political debate. Just as the age structure of the population that currently exists is primarily the result of individual choices we made in the past, individual decisions we make today will affect the nation tomorrow. We, each and all of us, decide whether to have children and form families (fertility rates), take care of our national health (mortality rates), to try to find jobs (labor force participation), leave one's home country and move to another country (immigration rate). These personal choices, when taken together, have a significant impact on the state of our economy—whether it grows or shrinks—and the taxes paid to our government. Collective individual choices as made today are not a drag on the economy but rather the anchor. We need to start looking at the results of our decisions in this context.

Notes

1. Sandra L. Colby and Jennifer M. Ortman, "Projections of the Size and Composition of the U.S. Population: 2014 to 2060," March 2015, U.S. Census Bureau, https://www.evernote.com/shard/s637/nl/121753408/c86b562c-56ec-4799-b10b -2b0464345390//res/0cae75d3-c6d7-4474-9977-ff8388621ffc/pop%20projections%20summary%20tables.pdf,

2. *America 2050*, "Demography Is Economic Destiny," http://www.america2050 .org/Pisano-Demography.pdf.

CHAPTER SEVEN

Implications for the Economy

The "Worker Gap" and Its Effect on Economic Growth and Unemployment

The purpose of the paint-by-numbers approach we have used in the preceding chapters is to represent visually two major demographic forces in American society, the baby boomers and Generation X. The pictures are useful models for examining the economic relationships among age, population, employment, retirement, and economic performance. When we connect the quantitative data and the qualitative features this data enumerates, we can perceive patterns and infer rules—for example, the relationships between demographic data and economic variables; the relationship between age and income over time. These can be plotted and graphed. The resulting portrait (also painted by the numbers) allows us to better understand the past, navigate the present, and prepare for the future. When the portraits of these two generations are compared side by side and tracked over time, a moving picture of the American economy emerges.

Analyzing pictures of a generation passing history, it becomes clear that our individual decisions, taken collectively, have major impacts on the economy. The size of these impacts is large, much larger than most of us would expect. So far we saw this reflected in the decline of the fertility rate; that is, we saw how the individual decisions to have fewer children or, in many cases, no children at all, fundamentally changed the U.S. economy. The collective consequence of birthing a smaller population means fewer people are able to work, achieve their highest earning potential and increase the nation's income; spend more money consuming products and services and growing demand; or pay money in taxes to government and support the public needs of the country. In other words, the result was a decline in economic growth and a decline in revenues paid to government.

In addition, we saw how individual attitudes toward changing our health care system, reducing risks to the environment and the human body, and generally emphasizing health and well-being over food, alcohol, and tobacco have, when taken collectively and coupled with advancements in medicine and medical technology, led to increasing our life expectancy and lowering the mortality rate.

Finally, we saw how individuals around the globe voluntarily decided, for a variety of reasons, to uproot their lives and migrate to the United States. When taken collectively, these individual decisions resulted in millions of new residents coming to the United States. We also saw how the perceived threat of these new arrivals—for example, their willingness to often work for lower wages than U.S. citizens—led to attitudes, laws, and policies that caused and continue to cause a reduction in the immigration rate, precisely at a time when the United States has a smaller population from which to draw its workforce. The United States is confronted with a classic example of Occam's razor where the simple approach of limiting (and for some, prohibiting) new immigrants will solve a perceived problem. As we think through and understand the complexity of the issue, and look at the all the consequences and the long-run implication of these actions, we see that the choice we are making is not necessarily the best decision in fact will be harmful. Rather, a complex solution involving a fuller understanding of issue with more effective outcomes, to be discussed in later chapters, will be required.

All of these personal decisions contributed to the transformation of the American people as a whole: a dramatic change in who we are, how many of us work, how many need pensions or welfare, and how much money we ultimately contribute to or take away from the national economy.

Furthermore, in the last chapter, we quantified, calculated, and predicted the likely impacts of our collective decisions on the future. The magnitude of the economic changes heading toward us may be surprising. Of course, these numbers are not the presentation of facts that we gathered while conducting field research in our time machine; rather, they are derived from the prism of collective decision making. They are a reflection of the decisions that we individually make, made possible by the world of big data. These numbers indicate what could happen, given a continuation of our collective behavior and existing economic and political policies.

The terrible truth is that it is entirely plausible that the future will be far worse than we have predicted so far, though we certainly hope it will not be (suggestions on how to change these impacts are discussed in the second part of this book). The analysis presented in this book only considers the direct effect of demographics on the economy and does not consider the multiplier effect that changes in income, consumption and taxes paid have the economy nor their impacts on the business cycle and dynamics of the economy. Proposals from presidential candidates, feedback from exit polls, the anti-immigration rhetoric in the Republican Party and the anti-business rhetoric and lack of proposals to fund promises in the Democratic Party, and the actual outcome of many presidential primaries all suggest that the future of the U.S. economy could be far worse than predicted. This chapter will continue to look at the economic consequences of demographic changes over time to evaluate the likely long-term results, *if we were to make no changes in policy or strategy.*

The opening chapter of this book described a perplexing and muddled economy: the closer you looked at the facts, the more confused you became. Nothing is more mysterious and strange than the current labor situation. How is it possible that we have thousands of jobs that we cannot fill, a 50 percent reduction of the unemployment rate and slow economic growth, yet the lowest labor participation rate in almost 40 years? In the past when we had a low unemployment rate, more often than not, this correlated with high economic growth. Our greatest concern during these periods was that inflation might be hard to tame. This was not what we experienced this time around. When the United States turned the corner on the Great Recession in 2010, the President's Council of Economic Advisors predicted robust economic growth of 3.9 percent over a five-year period and a reduction of the high unemployment rate of 10.8 percent to 5.9 percent.[1] The Obama administration's forecasters were not alone in their overly optimistic vision of the future. The Federal Reserve's forecast ranged from 4.5 percent to 3.5 percent economic growth for the same period. Only recently, in 2016, did the Federal Reserve finally relinquish its fantasy of a bright future when it predicted a growth rate of 1.8–2.2 percent for 2016–18.[2] Later that year, the financial forecasting units of most banks, firms, and universities followed suit, foreseeing consistent ranges at lower growth rates.

Contrary to everyone's predictions, more than five years after the Great Recession, we are struggling to maintain an average growth rate of 1.8 percent, which is less than half of the rate predicted in 2010. At the same time, the unemployment rate has plummeted further than anyone predicted to as low as 4.6 percent recently, which inverts the usual correlation. In a normal economy, declining unemployment rates would signal higher economic growth. What is the reason for this anomaly?

The best explanation for this unusual behavior is that demographic changes are working in concert with the age penalty. The boomers reached their maximum income in 2001 and then started to retire in 2010; while Generation X, a smaller population, entered the labor force. Less money was spent in two directions: people who are retiring earn less and spend less; and a smaller growth in the labor force means a smaller growth of population achieving their highest income, expenditures, and tax-paying years. To make matters worse, the boomers are starting to cost more money in health, pensions, and Social Security, while the population has the lowest labor participation rate in 38 years. This is the simplest and strongest explanation for the current confounding economic situation.

In the two decades prior to the millennium, the growth in working-age population averaged about 22 million new members per decade, while the number of retirees was much lower and declining at a rapid pace. Growth in the number of workers began to slow in the first decade of the century. In the current decade, we will average adding 9 million new members to the working-age population.[3] Ten years from now, many forecasters, including the U.S. Census, foresee 40 percent lower growth, with only 5 million new additions to the working-age population. (See Chapter 4 for a decade-by-decade breakdown of working-age population.) What is going on? What accounts for this precipitous decline?

Politicians have noticed. They blame one another. There is a basic disagreement among social scientists, journalists, and policy makers, who can find facts to support every argument. The most accurate facts are demographically driven. The fact is that the "prime working-age population"— that is, the age group of those most likely to work (ages 25–55)—is exhibiting the same slow growth as the past decade. The decline in the working-age population is only a part of the explanation. It helps explain how the unemployment rate has been steadily decreasing at a rate greater than the prediction of the most optimistic forecasters a decade ago, but it is not raising inflation or increasing growth. To understand, we need to turn to the effect of the age penalties on the economy.

The Great Recession arrived just as the transformation in demographics, communications, and computer technology changed the business world and society in general. The globalization of financial markets and the replacement of human resources by automated and robotic systems were among the many significant changes that have transformed how we live and work. Today, you can mail a message to a friend in Australia, buy a comic book in Japan, pay a bill, and attend traffic court for a moving violation you received from an automated traffic camera last month, all on your phone in a few hours. If you were born well before the advent of the Internet and smartphones, then you know how strangely futuristic this all sounds, but it is our current reality nonetheless. These inventions have changed the marketplace as well as our employment prospects: jobs were lost to answering services, ATM machines, traffic cameras, email, self-checkout at supermarkets, and so forth. The recovery period ran into the combined headwinds of these market forces. The changes in technology and automated systems occurred rapidly, driven by investment calculations and a surfeit of capital created by the nation's easing monetary policies. These policies accelerated investment decisions, generally not to labor's advantage. The demographic issues went unnoticed, but the storm they created lasted a long time. The unfortunate implications include the displacement of workers exacerbated by the fact that more jobs continue to move abroad.

The public and political backlash that has begun will undoubtedly continue to grow as more people become aware of these forces. When the economy did pick up, it was not surprising that even a rather sluggish level of job creation had the duel effect of pushing unemployment downward (beyond the expectation of our political leadership and the forecasts of most analysts): but, at the same time, the lack of a working-age population and employment opportunities did not create sufficient economic activity to propel growth and increase inflation.

It is important to note that the demographic penalty also generated a decline in consumption similar in size to the income penalty. If consumption is the major driver of economic growth and the average "consumption penalty" since 2010 has been $199.8 billion per year and averages $377 billion in constant 2015 dollars over the next 10 years, then consider the impact that having fewer people to buy goods and services each year on average contributes to dampening demand for all products across the board. This is a crucial and simple economic principle: aggregate demand drives consumption, which causes businesses to invest to meet this demand, resulting in economic growth. The hidden effect of the demographic consumption penalty is thwarting the behavior of $C+I+G\,(X-M)$. The main use of the surplus capital held by businesses over the past several years has been acquisitions and mergers and buying back their stock and not investing in plant and equipment. This in turn causes businesses not to invest in plants, equipment, and laborers; and, as a result, economic growth slows. It is no wonder that economic growth in the United States has been disappointing.

If the decline in the fertility rate of women and the deceleration of immigration that began a decade ago continues, we could be in serious trouble. The present political diatribes against immigration, with their incendiary rhetoric and support of discriminatory practices, needs to be reexamined, and solutions that will fully address Occam's razor crafted. And we must find alternative strategies to augment our workforce with individuals who have opted out for whatever reason. Otherwise, the indiscriminate reduction of our working-age population will continue to grow. The consequence of this would be a decrease in the growth of income and consumption on a national scale for decades to come, reminding us of the old adage: "be careful what you wish for."

The Age Penalty and the Decline of Annual Median Incomes and Income Inequality

One of the most commonly heard stump speeches from politicians, not only for the presidency but also for many other offices, is the claim that almost all Americans, save the upper 1 or 2 percent, have not received a pay increase in the past 15 years. In real terms (i.e., adjusted for inflation), the household median income has declined slightly from $57,843 in 1999 to $53,567 in 2014.[4] Recently the median income increased sharply to $56,500 but is still lower than 1999.[5] The official explanations for our income decreases are numerous. Some say, for example, that most manufacturing jobs were sent overseas as a result of global trade agreements and government regulations, leaving the men and women who used to do them with little other choice than jobs in the lower-paying service sector. (As mentioned at the end of Chapter 1, the vast majority of the jobs "added back" from the Great Recession were of this variety.) On the other hand, many Americans and some politicians, especially in the Republican Party, argue that the problem really comes down to our lack of border security and the influx of immigrants this allows. American citizens who worked in higher-paying labor industries like construction are worried about immigrants underbidding them on jobs or in the entry-level positions, working harder for less pay. Since the majority of immigrants come from countries where the cost of living is much lower, many Americans felt that these new arrivals squeezed them out of their industries or forced them to take jobs at rates that they never would have accepted before the recession. Meanwhile, economists, social scientists, and journalists pointed to another rival for U.S. jobs with which it was even harder to compete: technology. Since the advent of the Computer Age (also known as the Information Age, Digital Revolution, ad infinitum) technological invention and automation have replaced a diverse and lengthy list of jobs: bank tellers, book stores, gas station attendants, office managers, printers, secretaries, security guards, and supermarket staff, just to name a few. Still other Americans, often associated with the Democratic Party, point toward faulty policy that shifts income away from the general population to the upper-income elite, particularly those in the financial industry, who represent the notorious "2 percent." Due to increasingly necessary credit reviews, money has not flowed to smaller businesses and thus to those who operate or work for them.

While all these explanations legitimately contribute to the growing chorus of political claims that Americans have not had a raise in 15 years. There is another reason for the decline in the median income and changing demographics—specifically, the age distribution of the overall U.S. population and the financial penalty with it.

We present national income accounts in quintiles, not by age categories but rather by income distinctions, such as, upper, high, middle-high, middle, and low income. The following is an analysis of the 2000–2015 period in which Americans did not receive a salary increase. This calculation uses the paint-by-numbers approach. Table 7.1 presents the age cohort and the income gained for each. The first column describes the age groups; the second measures the change in the population size per each age category, with increases and decreases noted; and the third column is the change in the average per capita income as determined by the age income elasticity curve. The largest income increase occurs in the 15–35 years age group, yet there are only 4.25 million people added during this period, which reflects the baby boomers approaching old age and the smaller generation X coming of age. The 35–45 years age cohort had a decrease of 4.62 million people with a negative change of $7,600 per capita income. Cohorts that experience a decline in population generate less income, because they have fewer people generating income for that period. This is the net effect of the population structure change, the loss of income that is not realized for the 2000–2015 period. While the 45– to 55-year-old period has a larger gain in population, 6.5 million, their per capita increase is much smaller, $2,727. For the 55–65 age group, when boomers reached their maximum income and then began their descent into lower earnings, there were 16.6 million people with an average per capita decline of $4,636. The 65–75 age cohort had 9.2 million people, and their per capita income decline was $10,109. Finally, for those over 75 years, there was a 7.1 million population increase, and the cohort experienced an average per capita income decline of $10,625.

Table 7.1   The Age Penalty for Income and Consumption, 2000–2015

Age Cohort	Population Change during 2000–2015 (millions)	Income Change per Capita	Consumption Change per Capita
15–35 years	4,248	$12,680	$7600
35–45 years	(4,625)	$7,600	$5,000
45–55 years	5,450	$2,727	$545
55–64 years	16,629	$4,636	$3,182
64–75 years	9,203	$10,109	$6,250
>75 years	3,635	$10,625	$6,250

Overall, there was a net effect of 10.87 million people who made a positive addition to the national income over a 15-year period, while there were 37.6 million people who did not contribute income because of the change in the income age structure of their population cohort. When you do the simple arithmetic of summing these numbers, you come up with the age penalty for the period. Even though the population was increasing, those adding to the national economy were growing slower than those who did not and by a significant amount.

The age penalty here is caused by fewer people in the working-age population and more people whose incomes increase, and more people in the older age group whose incomes decrease. When these are combined, the decline in income growth is significant. Although there is growth in income, the rate of growth is 23.6 percent less than it would have been if population growth did not decline between generations. Since this penalty is an annual drop in income that compounds over time, its impact is exponentially higher.

The identical effect occurs when computing the compound interest rate of a loan. When you pay the interest for the first period of a loan, you add it to the total before calculating the interest for the second period, which is now bigger and so on. The total loan repayment increases in size over time due to the interest growth rate that accelerates faster and faster. The annual demographic penalty declines have the same exponential effect: the decline in growth for the nation for a 15-year period reaches a staggering negative $2.74 trillion, at an average $223 billion, altering the median income by $3,448 providing raises to all Americans lost per year as unrealized income. (Unrealized income is the sum of all of the changes in age composition and income of the 324 million people in the United States described above and the simple arithmetic of summing the changes. Thankfully, a computer model does this for us.) Keep in mind the effect of this demographic age structure change will continue for the next two decades and well beyond 2035 if the fertility rates, other policies that alter our working-age population, and immigration are not altered. Without changes, the sum of these impacts will double, and so on, compounding at an alarming rate until reaching overwhelming numbers.

Median household income is determined by looking at the distribution of all households incomes and finding the midpoint of the distribution. It is not surprising that Americans are not seeing a pay raise over this period; what is surprising, however, is the largest factor contributing to this. If the unrealized income, caused by the change in the population structure, were added to the calculation of the median income, the results would show an increase in the median income and positive annual income increases for working Americans. If we include the demographic income penalties amounting to $2.74 trillion for the period in the appropriate income quintiles and then compare the quintiles, while inequalities would still remain they would not be as pronounced.

The implications of the age dividend and the age penalty are numerous and far-reaching. Analysis of them can provide insight into our current economy, which is altering the political landscape in ways that are certainly not positive. Our best hope for change lies in the hands of the subject that demography studies: "We the People." By applying these demographic principles to economic analysis, we can develop new strategies to ensure our future economic health. This in turn would allow us to have productive political debates that we desperately need. We will return to this point in the chapters to come.

The Demographic Age Penalty for Consumption and Inflation

Consumption of goods and services is widely accepted as the primary driver of the gross national product both in the United States and abroad. Most economists agree that consumption is responsible for two-thirds of national growth and that, consequently, the consumer has driven the global economy for the past several decades. American consumers were one of the leading causes of global growth. So how does the demographic penalty change this dominant force?

Consumption increases if there is population and income growth. Clearly population has been increasing, so the cause of the lag in consumption is not slower population growth, but the change in the age distribution of that growth. Table 7.1 shows that this change in the composition of the population has a similar effect on consumption. The same number of net people in the 15-year period, 10.87 million, increased their consumption, and 37.6 million did not because of the same dynamics as the income increases and decreases resulting from the age demographic bonus and penalty.

The first 15 years of the century saw a 30 percent reduction in the rate of consumption, from 3.4 percent to 2.1 percent in the previous three decades. Each year there was a reduction in the growth of consumption that compounded and will grow substantially over the next several decades. The pattern of consumption reductions follows the same pattern as the unrealized income calculation described earlier and presented in Table 7.1, the last column. The total actual reduction in consumption for the period was over $985 billion–$79.3 billion average per year or $1.05 trillion per year. For the period leading up to the Great Recession, the reduction in the rate of consumption growth was a negative 1.1 percent and increased to a negative

14.8 percent. During and after the recession, there was a reduction in consumption as the reality of less income is realized and continues for decades.

Another way that consumption can increase is through assumption of debt, which is the explanation for the bubble that occurred at the turn of the millennium. Aside from the changes in the financial markets, which were documented in Chapter 1, there was a hidden change in income occurring. The world's largest financial institutions, banks with assets larger than some countries, overleveraged themselves and nearly went bankrupt by providing easier access to debt for homeowners, students, and even corporations. Most people thought the bursting of this bubble was the principal cause of the Great Recession. The slow-developing and long-lasting demographic penalty that really started to hit in 2001 gradually steered us toward the next contributing factor: lower income growth. Americans began to borrow more to maintain their purchasing habits. Ironically and tragically, this shift placed the responsibility of paying off the debt on those whose growth in incomes was declining: individuals with lower incomes who now had toxic mortgages. Regrettably, we are headed toward the same problem again since the decline in income and consumption will only increase over time creating a hazard for debt holders. This is a repetition of the debt cycle that we saw then and are beginning to see again. It will most likely have more serious ramifications on the nation's financial stability in the years to come if left unchecked.

Interestingly, the decline of the working-age population explains why forecasters underestimated the actual reduction of the unemployment rate that occurred. Since there was not a sufficient population participating in the workforce, when the economy picked up after the recession and the stimulus effect (described in Chapter 1) increased commerce and consumption, the unemployment rate was able to decrease beyond expectation, while growth did not increase to the predicted levels. Likewise, as the demographic penalties of both lower income and consumption began to kick in at the turn of the new millennium, the ensuing effect of less demand prevented prices from rising fast and kept inflation somewhat in check.

The sluggish growth of both our average incomes and consumption (and thus expenditures) is the principal source of our inability to recover fully from the Great Recession. We are now in one of the longest recovery periods since the Great Depression. Since macroeconomists do not typically use demographic characteristics in forecasting, they mostly did not foresee this hidden change, even though it has created a significant drag on our economy since 2001. These circumstances defy our classical assumptions of how capitalism really works at the macroeconomic level. On the other hand, corporate marketing departments are very sensitive to the economic conditions of their customers. They constantly predicate their decisions on listening to their customers and making corporate decisions on what they hear. The same should be true for our macroeconomic decisions—but where is the listening post other than government decision making? The key question is: have we reached the point when the scarcity of workers causes wages to increase to accelerate? The ultimate controlling dynamic is the inability of consumers to pay higher prices for goods given that their income growth is dampened by the demographic penalty. This is the "demographic income penalty" that we are now experiencing. In future years, the demographic penalties of income and consumption will grow and will continue for decades. The income penalty rises to a 24.7 percent reduction in annual growth over the next 20 years and, if we do not change our national policies, could last even longer. The same is also true for the consumption penalty, which grows at a 15.4 percent reduction in annual growth for the same period and likewise could also last beyond the next 20 years. This calls for a different set of strategies discussed in later chapters. The path we are on, at its core, is not working.

Productivity and Growth

There is another major component of national economic growth in addition to labor force growth and the availability of financial resources. It is productivity, particularly increases in labor and production established by inventions, innovations, and educational improvements in the work force. The general public perception in the digital age is surprisingly bolstered by the belief that technology is the answer to all our economic woes. There are several authors who are challenging this basic assumption. First, Robert J. Gordon's recently published work, *The Rise and Fall of American Growth*, provides an excellent survey of productivity growth in the last century as well as a glimpse of the probable future. The second is Marc Levinson, *An Extraordinary Time: The End of the Postwar Boom and the Return of the Ordinary Economy,* who argues that recovery after World War II, described as the "Golden Age," resulted from a set of unusual circumstances that raised unrealistic expectations of Americans' that cannot be replicated in the future.[6] Both authors essentially argue that the past 70 years are one-off opportunities, that the Industrial Revolution itself was a one-off in modern economic history that shaped the developed world as we understand it, and there is a return to world that existed after the agricultural revolution, a world with slow and possibly no real growth albeit with higher levels of technology and higher levels of wealth creation. This story of productivity adds another level of intrigue to our thoroughly enigmatic economy. Given the rapid pace of technological innovation, the amount of capital invested in it, and the visibility of the digital, communications, and robotics era, which Gordon refers to as the Third Industrial Revolution (2004–2014), one would expect that technology would be the answer to the creeping pace of labor force growth..

Gordon distinguishes the pace of innovation from the impact of innovation on the growth rates of labor productivity. He looks at total factor productivity (TFP), which can be defined as the impact of technological change on the real GDP divided by a weighted average of labor and capital input. Gordon focuses on what labor and capital are doing to increases in GDP—and not just the frenzy of capital spending on invention. This distinction helps explain why the recent investment in social media technologies between 2004 and 2014, roughly the same period as the demographic transition, yielded a scant productivity increase of less than half of a percent (0.4 percent) per year as opposed to the nearly 2 percent (1.89 percent) increase per year of the post–World War II period and the over 1 percent (1.03 percent) during the dot-com period (1994–2004). Both overlapped with the demographic transformation that we are experiencing today.[7]

Gordon found that the recent contribution of productivity was as disappointing as the findings of his analysis of the growth of the labor force. Concerning technology, he believes that the rapid technological changes mentioned earlier have now succumbed to a long slow period of growth, recognizing the difficulty of predicting what new tech inventions and innovations will occur in the future. The time period of these industrial revolutions occurred simultaneously with the arrival of the demographic age penalty. A pair of logical question follows: Does this demographic penalty alter the results of the productivity calculations? Did the drag of the demographic penalties described in this chapter alter the effectiveness of the calculations? Since the real GDP that Gordon uses in his calculations does not include the "unrealized GDP income" of $3.35 trillion–$223 billion average per year (between 2004 and 2014) caused by the age distribution of our population, does it alter Gordon's TFP ratio (total factor productivity) if it is included in the calculation? Clearly it should—and by a substantial amount. The population is the same in both calculations, of course, but the GDP would be different and not by a small amount. If this figure were included in our calculations, the productivity would certainly be higher. Again, it is possible that the significant role that people and their individual behavior collectively—demographically—have on the economy is the dynamic that actually is the driver of the economy. Even more intriguing is the thought that the technology of people, through the relationship of organizations in society through changes in the rules of game (Douglass North's hypothesis), can be the altering force of human history.

If you are still wondering whether the penalty could be that large, a quick scan in real time illustrates the plausibility of this impact. In the first years of the decade (2000–10), when boomers were reaching their highest earing period of $4,636 more per person than the previous period, there were 5 million fewer in the working-age population, and in the next decade there were more than 11 million fewer. In the same period, there were 5 million more retirees whose incomes was $10,109 less per person; and, in the next decade, there will be 16 million more retirement-aged persons entering the population, with $10,625 less per person. When simple arithmetic on these cohorts and all the other cohorts is performed and compounded, the size of the penalty $223 billion, becomes real dollars that are not included in the economy. If this penalty is included in the calculation of productivity, the answer will be quite different.

One additional thought about the role of productivity is the impact of technology on innovation on the economy, according to Gordon. It might be that the transfer from invention to innovation has not completed its cycle and that the institutional change and transfer from invention to innovation has not yet occurred. The insights of Joseph Schumpeter, considered the father of entrepreneurialism, casts light on the distinction. The difference between an inventor and innovator is that an inventor invents, whereas an innovator scratches an itch or problem that society has, and the innovation changes society. Thus, the invention not only goes viral, but creates robust economic activity over the long run, leading to growth. When innovation is looked at from this perspective, the results are hopeful for the future (and will be discussed in Chapter 9).

There is another interesting question to be asked. The Third Industrial Revolution and the post period of 2004–14[8] occurred in the same time as the reorientation of the economy from a production-oriented to an individual consumer–based economy. In this latter economic framework, consumer surplus (i.e., increased consumer satisfaction) should be considered complementary to increased output per person per hour of work. The Information Age we are now in makes this possible. The Information Age empowerment of individuals to make individual decisions and shop the world market, thus getting better prices and diversity of products, actually increasing the bundle of products as well, leads to greater consumer satisfaction. Does the convenience of more options for communicating and networking have a value (the price and value comparison)? What this revolution has created may not directly increase productivity measured as output per man-hour, but is it as valuable, if not more valuable, to the consumer? Going forward, the question of what we look at and what we measure will need to reflect both who the subject is and what the object is that we are measuring and using to judge our economic performance. If the decision maker is the individual consumer, then finding ways of measuring consumer surplus will need to be part of the economic calculus.

Notes

1. Council of Economic Advisors, *Economic Report of the President 2010* (Washington D.C.: Government Printing Office, 2010), p. 75.

2. Ben Leubsdorf, "U.S. Comes to Grips with Slow Growth," *Wall Street Journal*, January 20, p. R4, http://www.wsj.com/articles/after-7-years-of-slow-growth-u-s-now-sees-more-of-same-1453239179.

3. These numbers are derived from data shared in Chapter 4.

4. Mark J. Perry, "Update: How Changing Household Composition, Household Work Hours, and Retirement Explain Median Household Income," *Seeking Alpha*, March 6, 2016, http://seekingalpha.com/article/3956204-update-changing-household-composition-household-work-hours-retirement-explain-median.

5. Binyamin Appelbaum, "Incomes in U.S. Are Up Sharply; Poor Gain Most," *New York Times*, September 14, 2016.

6. Marc Levinson, *An Extraordinary Time: The End of the Postwar Boom and the Return of the Ordinary Economy* (New York: Basic Books, 2016).

7. Robert J. Gordon, *The Rise and Fall of American Growth* (Princeton, NJ: Princeton University Press, 2016), p. 505.

8. Gordon, *The Rise and Fall of American Growth*.

CHAPTER EIGHT

Implications for Government Budgets

Existing Use of Demographics in Government Budgeting

Many of the programs, investments, and policies of government have long-term implications. They are the result of a decision-making process that is slow and time-consuming. By its very nature, the period of analysis needs to be longer. As we think about the consequences of growth decisions, we need to understand what will happen to people in the long run. Demographic analysis in infrastructure and natural environment decisions has been a mainstay of the demographic process. In fact, many innovations in the field of demography have evolved from this work. Likewise, in many policy areas—such as housing, economic development, land use planning, and many others—demographic analysis has been a mainstay of analysis and decision making.

But in other circumstances when money is on the table—for example, for budgets with personnel and operational issues—the time frame for analysis changes. These are looked at as short-term issues even though they have long-term implications. For these issues, demographic analysis is either not done or done as an afterthought. Moreover, when demographics are considered in the budget process, a description of the characteristics (number, composition, gender, ethnicity, age, etc.) of the population is usually as far as the analysis goes. The impact of people on the economy and the funding implications, particularly the long-run effects (which have been the focus of the previous chapters), are not considered.

There are exceptions. The Federal Budget Act established the Congressional Budget Office to do a long-term budget assessment; in doing so, it looks at the demography of the country. Its budget, based on a long-run demographic profile, is an example that it can be done. Additionally, the independent Government Accountability Office (GAO), the nation's auditor, undertakes a long-run report on federal, state, and local finances. But even its analysis would benefit from the demographic bonus and penalty work described in this book.

Other governmental units in the country do not prepare long-term, demographic-based financial analysis that considers the impact of demographic changes on the economy and finances of a jurisdiction. Most government budgets are annual budgets. But in this period of fiscal stress, budgets can change in the course of a year, necessitating adjustments in order to achieve a balanced budget, a requirement the Constitution places on states and their subdivisions, local governments. Today the primary cause of existing and projected financial shortfalls is demographic change that increases expenditures on pensions and health care, other post-employment benefits, and deferred maintenance of capital investments. These expenditures exceed current revenue sources, including federal transfers. The projected shortfalls do not consider the impacts that the same demographic changes will have on the economic picture of the nation, nor do they consider the revenue side of the equation, which will also substantially increase the budget shortfalls. The GAO is now undertaking this analysis.

A Millennium Issue for Government

Case studies of local and state governments conducted by the George Mason School of Public Policy, the University of Southern California Price School of Public Policy, the University of San Francisco, and the Volker Institute assess how state and local governments are dealing with increasing fiscal stress. Among the conclusions of all the case studies is the lack of long-term fiscal analysis in budget analysis, presentation, and deliberations. Only a few jurisdictions look beyond 5 years in their budget analysis, and even fewer look out to 10 years. Some state and local entities did rely on national CBO long-term economic forecasts, but their local and state demographic and fiscal forecasts look solely at population growth forecasts and not at the economic consequences of demographic change.

The California case studies includes this observation from a high-level member of the advisory board: the "continual fiscal pressure that local governments are facing and the difficulty of making these decisions will be the greatest challenge facing our democratic system." The member notes that meeting the fiscal demands of all our special interests in a long period of fiscal austerity will be an overwhelming task for all jurisdictions and will test our democratic system.[1]

The GAO does prepare a report of the long-run picture of state and local government finances, looking out to 2050. The analytical model is based on demographic changes over time and includes a cost structure of all government expenditures for all goods and services that government provides on the expenditure side. The revenue side does not include any demographic analysis that could alter future revenue sources based on demographic changes described in earlier chapters. Rather, revenue sources derived from existing tax policies are calculated based on unchanging demographic assumptions. Both expenditures and revenues consider the variations due to geography at the state and local levels. This analysis was directed by Congress to understand the implications that federal transfer payments are having on state and local finances. This exceptional review of all state and local budgets included 50 state governments and 87,525 local governments. These local governments include 3,034 county governments, 19,429 municipal governments, 16,504 townships, 13,506 school districts, and 35,052 special districts. The total expenditures for state and local governments are 14 percent of the national GDP. Their operating deficit between revenues and expenditures is over 1 percent of GDP and would require a 5 percent reduction in spending or a similar increase in revenues to eliminate it. The major reasons for the funding gap are the pension and health costs for government employees and states' continuing health costs for Medicare. The major driver of these increased costs is changing demography, particularly the increasing number of retirees; pension programs that are not fully funded; and increasing health costs of older populations. Prior to the Affordable Health Care Act, the funding gap was as high as 14 percent in 2012.[2]

When infrastructure needs for our states and local governments are added to the fiscal picture, the funding gap gets much larger. Over the past several decades, as public entities have faced fiscal pressure, deferred maintenance needs and/or replacement of infrastructure has significantly increased. Additionally, spending on infrastructure needs has not kept up with the rise in population and the growth needs of the country. Conservative estimates to refurbish our aging infrastructure, mostly built in the last century, and address immediate growth needs until 2020 are well over $3.6 trillion. The engineers and designers of the system, ASCE, give us a D+ grade.[3] Adding the federal budget picture shows the full picture and makes clear that fiscal sustainability of government is the millennial issue, according to George McCarthy of the Lincoln Institute of Land Policy.[4] Thankfully, the work of the CBO and the GAO gives a clearer picture of the federal challenge, but even their analysis does not fully account for the longer-run demographic analysis on revenues. This has been widely discussed in the press and the ongoing political dialogue of the country. Interestingly, it was not widely discussed in the 2016 presidential campaign. In fact, most of the dialogue, from both parties, centered on measures that would substantially add to the size of the federal debt. The U.S. debt now stands at $18 trillion and will add $544 billion or 2.9 percent of GDP in 2016.[5] Congress has been struggling to keep the budget from increasing over the past several years; however, political interests and elections have postponed dealing with the major reason for the cost increases: entitlements of health (Medicare and Medicaid) and Social Security. The debate among economists and business leaders on whether the size of the deficits is a cloud on the growth of the country is one of the most perplexing issues in the country today.

Currently the best friend that the deficit has is the low interest rate, the result of our current "easy money" monetary policy. How long that lasts and how the political process deals with the deficit issue is anybody's guess. Jeffery Miron of Harvard University estimates that the long-run debt over 75 years expressed in the present value of U.S. expenses exceeds the present value of revenues by a very large amount: $117.9 trillion.[6] This estimate is based on all policies and assumptions remaining in place in the future.

The Unraveling of America's Fiscal Sustainability: A Steep Hill to Climb

When the demographic age penalty of taxes paid to government, described in the previous chapter, is added to the fiscal stress facing all levels of government, the fiscal hill becomes steeper and longer. This penalty is created by the same dynamics: a slower growth in working people and, in some periods, actually a smaller number of people paying more taxes. At the same time, many more older people are paying lower taxes. While tax revenues will be growing over the next decades, the growth rate will be half of what it was the last *three* decades of the 21st century. The Bureau of Economic Analysis's historical report on the growth rate of taxes paid shows that the age penalty reduction of taxes paid is actually happening. Income, sales, property, gasoline, cigarette, and 12 other tax categories paid by individuals grew by 3.8 percent over the 1970–2000 period; in the 2000–2015 period, their growth rate was 1.7 percent.[7]

The actual size of the penalty is calculated using the same method described in the previous chapter to calculate the income and consumption penalties. The data is presented in Table 8.1. The first column in the

Table 8.1   Demographic Penalty for Taxes Paid, 2000–2015

Ages	Changes in Population (millions)	Changes in Taxes Paid per Capita Federal/State/Local
15–35	4,248	$14/$44/$22
36–45	(4,625)	$169/$143/$14
46–55	5,450	$327/$85/$28
56–65	16,629	$593/$101/$46
66–75	9,203	$415/$159/$89
75>	3,635	$448/$74/$81

table is the age cohort, the second column is the change in the population in each age cohort during 2000–2015, and the third column is the increase or decrease in the taxes paid by the age group in the period. If the population grew in the age group and the taxes paid rose, there would be an increase in taxes paid for that age cohort. The reverse is also true: if the population or the taxes paid decreased for the period, there would be a decrease in taxes paid for the cohort.

The analysis showed that 10.86 million people did contribute more taxes, which are broken out among federal, state, and local governments; and 37.6 million people paid fewer taxes for federal, state, and local governments and other fees, including severance and license. When the calculations for all 324 million people in the country are made for each year and the annual rates are then compounded over the period, all governmental agencies in the United States in the past 15 years received $2.2 trillion–$146.8 billion average per year. It is no wonder that the government has been facing fiscal stress. Two-thirds or more of the annual penalty is at the federal level, and the rest falls on the local levels of government that cannot rely on deficit spending to deal with budget shortfalls. They must either cut services or raise revenues. Looking forward, the age penalty of taxes paid increases. The growth rate of revenue for the period 2015–2035 decreases 45.8 percent.

These reductions in revenue growth and the increasing costs into the future create a very steep fiscal hill that is quickly approaching for government.

Those who are involved in budgeting know that the most sensitive variable is the growth in new revenues. The taxes-paid demographic penalty, like the income and consumption penalties, will increase substantially over the next two decades as more of the boomers retire. If the fertility and immigration rates continue to decline, these penalties could continue indefinitely. The collective impact of demography on government is both increasing expenditures and decreasing revenues, given current policies and tax rates and structures. The adoption of new taxes and increases in tax rates will be politically difficult to pass when the growth of income is also decreasing. Asking voters to increase taxes when their incomes are not growing robustly and their consumption growth rate is similarly not growing as expected presents a steep hill for government to climb. It is no wonder that the political process is showing signs of unraveling in America today. It will get worse over the next decades.

It is also not surprising that the 2016 presidential race brought out voters across the country who are angry and frustrated. For example, in the Pennsylvania primary, a closed primary where voters could only vote for candidates in their party, 61,500 Democrats changed parties to vote for a Republican. "Many of them are Reagan Democrats: white, working class, blue collar, incomes of $35,000 to $40,000 or less, high school education or less. They feel frustrated, they felt left behind," said G. Terry Madonna, a professor at Franklin and Marshall College in Lancaster, Pennsylvania. The cause of the frustration is an interesting question. Is it the change in the economic base, the demographic age structure, an increase in taxes, or all the above?[8] It will be difficult for government to deal with the political dynamic resulting from increasing public good needs and declining revenues in a political environment where income is not growing.

How Does Government Deal with Declining Resources?

Even with the arrival of the tax-lowering Proposition 13 mentality in California that swept across the country in the late 1970s, Americans increased their support for public expenditures, particularly at the federal level. As discussed in previous chapters, in the three decades prior to the millennium, the growth in taxes paid was 3.8 percent. This clearly showed a willingness of Americans to pay more for public goods and services. Since then, the growth has been 1.8 percent. Clearly the reduction of tax growth rate by over 50 percent is crimping how government does business. From the case study work, it became apparent that the government has deferred expenditures in low-visibility areas such as maintenance, while funding pensions, health care and other post-employment benefits as best they could with uneven fiscal performance across the country. In addition, governments have also funded many capital investments using municipal bonds or general obligation bonds that have used demographic forecasts based on higher growth rates that are not likely to be realized when you take into account the full range of impacts from these demographic changes. This raises the likely specter that municipal debt may not be as secure as once thought and/or that government will be faced with higher debt financing costs depending on the finance instrument.

The growth rate of the economy and, even more important, the growth rate of future revenues are key assumptions in the budgeting process for all levels of government. Because many of the costs are fixed in public budgets, revenue growth rates are used as the strategy to balance budgets. Unfortunately, the reality of the age penalty challenges these assumptions.

Beginning in 2010, the impact of the demographic penalty shows the growth rate of taxes paid by individuals to local, state, and federal governments declining by 45.8 percent in the future. Since personal taxes account for 85 percent of all federal, state, and local revenues, these age penalty reductions will, over the next 20 years, have a significant impact on government budgets, at all levels, for a very long time.

Notes

1. "Southern California Fiscal Sustainability and Governance Project," Report to the John Randolph Haynes and Dora Haynes Foundation, June 2014.

2. Government Accountability Office, "2016, Government Fiscal Outlook" https://help.evernote.com/hc/en-us/articles/209005347.

3. "Report Card for Americas Infrastructure," American Society of Civil Engineers, 2015, http://www.infrastructurereportcard.org/economic-impact/.

4. George W. McCarthy, "Lincoln Institute CEO Discusses Cities' Challenges to Sustain Solvency," presentation to University of Southern California, Price School of Policy, March 2015, https://priceschool.usc.edu/lincoln-institute-ceo -discusses-cities-challenges-to-sustain-solvency/.

5. "The Deficit Rises Again," *Wall Street Journal*, Review & Outlook, January 2016, http://www.wsj.com/articles/the-deficit-rises-again-1453768153

6. Jeffery Miron, *US Fiscal Imbalances* (Washington, D.C.: Cato Institute, 2016).

7. Bureau of Economic Analysis, "Income Sources and Expenditures Accounts, 2016," http://www.bea.gov/national/Index.htm.

8. Lisa Mascaro, "East Coast Primaries: Trump and Clinton Have Strong Nights while Sanders Edges Away from White House Bid," *Los Angeles Times*, April 26, 2016.

CHAPTER NINE

Long-Term Growth in America

Relationship of Demography to Fiscal and Monetary Policy Tools

The implications of the age dividend and the age penalty are far-reaching, and they have not been recognized or understood. Because of their hidden nature, many citizens who are affected by them—a large percentage of the American people—unknowingly experience them, adversely feel their effects, and are looking for someone to make things better. Our leaders are also affected and equally in the dark. The result is a lot of finger pointing about why the economy is not working. This has been happening for a number of years. It may be one of the reasons, as we look for someone to blame, for the turmoil in our political processes. Therefore, it is important to understand what the impacts are and how they relate to our policy instruments so our elected and administrative leaders can understand what can be done. What strategies could work? Even more important, what role could we play in dealing with our current circumstances and our future economic health?

In light of the demographic findings of earlier chapters, this chapter will look at how fiscal and monetary policies could stimulate growth. The previous chapters provided a calculation of the demographic bonuses and penalties for income, consumption and taxes paid. The size of the bonuses and penalties were probably a surprise to most readers. The focus of this chapter is their collective effect on the nation's GDP and how they relate to the fiscal and monetary policies put into effect over the past two decades. The period experienced the recession of 1990–1991 and the Great Recession of 2007–2009. We will need to isolate the impacts of the recessions and cyclical impacts from the demographic impacts.

The decade of 1990–2000 is called the "Goldilocks economy"—"The Fabulous Decade" by Janet Yellen and Alan Binder.[1] The economy performed on all cylinders, growing at an ideal 4 percent increase in GDP. Productivity doubled to 2.8 percent from the previous decade; unemployment dropped from 7.8 percent to 4.1 percent, considered the ideal target; and inflation was held in check at 2.9 percent in a hot economy. Couldn't be better. These authors suggest that all branches of government made all the right moves. President Clinton submitted tight budgets. Congress passed tax increases. Alan Greenspan eased the money supply and then, at the right moment, tightened interest rates to prevent inflation from undermining the growth party. Business, reeling from the double impacts of the recession and the advent of free trade with foreign competition, *began* a massive restructuring of the way business operates. Industry clusters and the logistics supply system were developed, and the rest is history. The last half of the decade when all this was done was as good as it can be. Some say that the sun, stars, and moon were aligned; others call it luck. Many Republicans argued that it was the delayed impact of the Reagan tax cuts.

One element was missing from the equation. The demographic bonus of the baby boomers was at its peak, as we remember from Chapter 6 (see Figure 6.1). They made a significant contribution to the growth of the economy: growing incomes by 15.2 percent; raising productivity by adding unanticipated income to national income accounts with the same number of workers; and increasing demand by adding 10.7 percent to expenditures/consumption.[2]

The best way to think of this dynamic in the demographic bonus era is to look at the changes in the demographic makeup of the population between the decades. If there were more people, making more money than the previous period, and there were fewer people actually entering retirement who were making less, then more national income would be generated. Since econometric models and forecasts do not consider these aging changes over time, they would not capture this bonus. One could suggest that President Clinton, Congress, and Alan Greenspan had the good fortune of implementing their policies at the same time that the boomers started reaching their stride in the labor force.

Using the method described in Chapter 5 to calculate the size of the demographic dividend, a bonus of $22.5 billion was directly pumped into the economy in 1997, $57.7 billion in 1998, and $102.7 billion in 1999. Over $182.9 billion was added in the three year period, and it went directly into income and consumption. This was almost a quarter of the program put into effect to stimulate the recovery from the Great Recession, and the economy was more than 30 percent smaller. The demographic dividend had the effect of pumping more dollars into the economy at the same time as monetary and fiscal policy went into effect. This created a synergy that made the economy hum. The increased money went directly into expenditures by consumers. There were no shovel-ready projects, no transfers through the financial institutions. The stimulus of the demographic bonus does not detract from the leadership initiatives taken, but it shows the importance of understanding what "We the People" can contribute to the economy. That the government policies maintained a calm course without understanding this hidden dynamic is even more laudable.

The millennium started a new demographic chapter as the bonus turned into a penalty when the boomers' income started to decline in 2001. But the history of tax cuts as a positive stimulus did not repeat itself as we encountered the recession of 2001. President Bush used tax cuts as a stimulator with the Economic Growth and Tax Relief Acts of 2001 and 2003; President Obama continued both to 2013. But the undetected demographic bonus quietly went neutral and started a shift to a penalty as the boomers reached their maximum earning period in 2001. Their incomes started to decline, which coincided with the recession of 2001–2002. No dividend bonus was injected into the economy. In fact, there was a hidden unrealized income penalty of $1.05 trillion for the decade that coincided with the Great Recession. It is during this period that we see the full effect of the fiscal policies of the American Recovery and Restoration Act and the monetary policies of Bernanke and Yellin, the policies that are in place today. The economy stabilized, but the recovery has been slow and the longest recovery of any postwar recession, the demographic penalty blunted the policies attempted.

We find our country mired in the perplexing state described in Chapter 1 where nothing seems to work. We also find ourselves mired in political solutions that at best will not address the fundamental issues facing the nation and worse could actually exacerbate our problems. Our political candidates, unaware of these demographic implications, propose solutions that do not address the basic issue behind our economic dilemma. No one is talking about "us" and our demographic contribution to the solution. If we look at the demographic penalty over the next five years, the period of the next administration and the next election cycle, the penalties get much larger, so large that to ignore them is folly. Currently the income penalty for the period is $2.56 trillion–$673 billion per year; the consumption penalty is $1.22 trillion–$290 billion per year. As the boomers retire in large numbers and labor force growth trails behind, the penalties will increase over the next two decades. Even more problematic is the taxes-paid penalty $1.27 trillion–$329 billion per year which could be added annually to the budget deficit.

Demography and Long-Term Economic Growth

In the future, the demographic cycle will also dampen long-term growth. Previous chapters discussed the effect of changes in the cycle on consumption, investment, and government, in every part of the $C+I+G$ equation these penalties do not bode well. The United States is not the only nation experiencing a changing demographic pattern. So do most of the industrial nations and some far more impacted. Japan, almost all of Europe, East and West, and now even many of the developing nations are experiencing this demographic pattern. So if we expect to turn to imports and exports $(X-M)$ as the solution to our economic objectives, we are likely to be disappointed. The future does not look promising. For those who think the answer to growth is increasing money in circulation to be made available for investment, this pathway is not promising unless consumption is increasing, which would require more investment. The Federal Reserve has been pursuing this strategy in the past several years, and, as mentioned, it will not increase the appetite of the growth machine. When tax reductions were synergized with the demographic cycle, they were effective. But by themselves the results were disappointing. It would be folly to assume that growth will occur by cutting taxes. Furthermore, given the effect of the demographic penalty on reducing taxes paid and the likelihood of disappointing growth not only for the economy but also for growth in taxes paid, this strategy will add to the federal deficit. Fiscal initiatives to stimulate economic growth, on the other hand, will cause deficits, which are high now, to grow larger. It is fair to say that our current policies need an assist, will reducing regulations be sufficient?

Over the past several decades, the evidence of demographics' impact on the economy is clear. It is important to look at these impacts as we plot our economic course. They should be included in political deliberations and decisions. Neither tax cuts nor increased federal spending is the answer. The economic growth debate needs to be looked at in light of the reality that the decision maker in this century is "We the People" speaking for "We the Economy." An important consideration in our decisions on political candidates at all levels of government, is whether they are listening to us, know what we are doing to the economy, and whether they are putting forth policy proposals that relate to our economic behavior.

Labor Force Population Growth and Economic Growth

Simultaneously, another demographic problem is also having a dampening effect on long-term economic growth: the shrinking size of the working-age population that is the source of our labor force. Historically, labor force growth has contributed up to two thirds of our GDP growth. From the years of 1970–2000, for example, the baby boomers entered the labor force and the age dividend began. A larger percentage of our population was of working age, which led to higher GDP growth. Other salient factors were at play during this period, including the increase in the number of women entering the labor force, and the rise in popularity of tech products.

Nonetheless, the influence of labor force growth on GDP growth can be seen in Figure 9.1. As the chart shows, when boomers entered the labor force, the United States had an annual labor force growth rate of 2.7 percent. The boomers' high-income growth years (35–55 years old) occurred between 1980 and 2000 when the GDP growth rate rose to 3.1–3.2 percent. In contrast, the 2000–2010 labor force growth rate of 0.5 percent was the smallest since 1930; and, worse, it is predicted to crawl along even more slowly over the next two decades, as shown in Figure 9.1. When the labor force began to shrink and the age penalty arose, declines in incomes and expenditures, coupled with the deleveraging of the Great Recession, generated a 1.8 percent GDP growth rate for the decade. We see in Figure 9.1 that the growth of the working-age population is reduced in half, which is continuing to today and will continue for decades, creating a "workers' gap." The workers' gap describes a shortage within the working-age population, which will slow the growth of the economy. Without a change in policy and strategy, the workers' gap could generate even lower GDP growth. Those who suggest that we can return to the growth rates of the past without dealing with labor force population growth are ignoring the real force driving our economy, "We the People."

Think about this. Our labor force primarily comes from our working-age population. While our current policies are focused on the unemployment rate of this population, the demographic cycle is gradually changing the number of working-age people available to it. Since the number of people in the generations following the baby boomers is significantly smaller, the rapid retirement of boomers at a rate of roughly 10,000 people per day reaching retirement age, establishes a deficit in our labor force population. GenX, the generation after the boomers, is smaller than the Millennial generation, which is larger than GenX but smaller than the boomers. Now entering the labor force, it will not pick up the slack. Couple this with the lower fertility rates of our domestic population, including recent immigrants, and the reduction in the number of foreign-born immigrants, we have a labor shortage crisis that will continue for decades. Figure 9.1 shows that projected employment growth rates over the next few decades will be less than half the rate of the past several decades.

What is conclusive about a real-time examination of demography and economic growth today is the decline in the working-age population, from which the labor force is derived. Not only is it declining or increasing at a slower rate, but, making matters worse, it is declining in many of the higher-income age categories.[3] When the income associated with these changes is considered, there are large and measurable negative impacts on economic performance (i.e., less growth in national income), and productivity increases are not as robust as anticipated. Thus, growth rates are continually over-stated not only by the Council of Economic Advisors but also the Federal Reserve most private sector forecasters and most recently by the incoming administration.

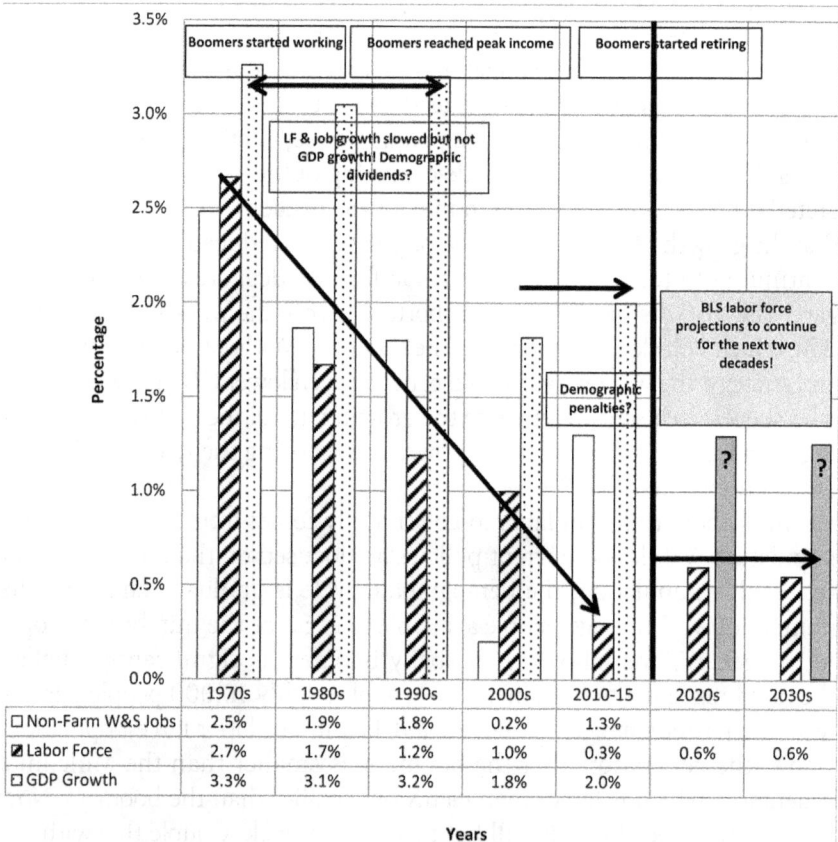

	1970s	1980s	1990s	2000s	2010-15	2020s	2030s
☐ Non-Farm W&S Jobs	2.5%	1.9%	1.8%	0.2%	1.3%		
☑ Labor Force	2.7%	1.7%	1.2%	1.0%	0.3%	0.6%	0.6%
☐ GDP Growth	3.3%	3.1%	3.2%	1.8%	2.0%		

Years

Figure 9.1   "Workers Gap" Jobs, Labor Force and GDP Growth

Note: The GDP growth in the 1920s and 1930s would be lower than past decades.

Sources: Population, U.S. Census, 2014 Population Projection; workers, Bureau of Labor Survey and Census Population Survey 2015.

When the consumer demographic penalty is included, the slow-growing and perplexing economy comes into clearer focus. When the income demographic penalty-$2.56 trillion, and consumption penalty-$1.22 trillion, for the next four years are considered, achieving even current growth may be difficult to achieve. Add the demographic tax penalty of $1.27 trillion of unrealized taxes for the four year period, along with promised tax reductions, which could increase the debt, could make it even more difficult to grow the economy without different policy strategies. The continued compounding effect of all the demographic penalties and the emergence of the workers' gap, the non transparent result of our collective individual decisions, are the underlying forces that must be considered to achieve desired growth.

Comparison of Economic Base Change and Age Change on the Economy

Another chorus sung on the political stumping ground is that America has lost manufacturing jobs to our international competitors. Some suggest that these jobs have been "stolen." Whatever the reason, the global playing field has reduced good-paying jobs in the United States, and this situation has contributed to our economic malaise. The record bears this out. The peak of manufacturing jobs was 1979 with 19.4, million jobs and the number has fallen ever since to 11,528 in 2009 and now stands at 12,238 million jobs.[4] There has been resurgence since the height of the Great Recession, the result of a regeneration effort on the part of industry (described in Chapter 10), showing that the United States, with the right growth strategy, can successfully compete and grow good jobs despite foreign competition.

If we compare the income from the lost jobs in manufacturing with the income from the service sector and other jobs that have replaced them, the difference is $24,440 per job in constant 2013 dollars. The chorus of complaints is well placed. Our free trade adventure has not been accompanied by a job creation strategy. At the same time, our economy has also been dealing with the demographic transformations that have actually inflicted greater negative impacts on the economy.

Looking at the total job losses in the period 2000 to present, the free trade era, 4.46 million jobs were lost, each with a loss of $24,440.[5] Now compare that loss with the 37.6 million people who realized an unearned income loss of $7,051 due to the changing demographic structure. The simple arithmetic calculation shows that the demographic penalty had a 243 percent larger impact on the economy than the losses from free trade, since the millennium. Just as we need a strategy to deal with economic regeneration in order to increase the number of higher-paying jobs, we have an ever-greater need to have a strategy to deal with the negative effects of the workers' gap and the demographic age penalties.

There is also a positive way of looking at the penalty: we have 37.6 million more people who are living longer and enjoying the economic benefits of the improvements in medicine and their personal good lifestyle decisions. These societal benefits need to be weighed when evaluating the public policy implication of the demographic age penalty.

We will need new policy tools, new strategies, and new ways of doing business to understand these demographic penalties and change the way we do our economic business. At the center of the discussion will be the need to look more carefully at who "We the People" are—in particular, the working-age population. The pressing issue in the near future will not be unemployment, but rather the scarcity of available labor and the need to reduce structural unemployment and working age population not participating in the economy. We need to figure out how to use people we have written off. We cannot make the mistake of preventing those who can contribute to the economy from coming here. Ironically, adding to the working-age population will be most significant economic issue in the future.

Equally as problematic will be finding new ways of creating a living environment that encourages our individual collective choice decisions to benefit the whole. How can we alter our fertility rate? How can we use the decline in our mortality rate, which results from both improvements in medicine and reductions in environmental risks, to overcome the growing intergenerational divide in the country? How can we organize ourselves to increase the productivity of our scarce resource—people? These penalties of unrealized income, consumption, and taxes paid will require new and different strategies, to be discussed which is the subject matter of Part 2 of this book.

Notes

1. Alan S. Binder and Janet L. Yellen, *The Fabulous Decade: Macroeconomics Lessons from the 1990s* (New York: Century Foundation Press, 2001).

2. America 2050, "Demography Is Economic Destiny," http://www.america2050.org/Pisano-Demography.pdf.

3. Data in Chapter 4 indicates that the 35–44 and 45–54 age cohorts—the higher-income growth years—are having the slowest increases in population.

4. Bureau of Labor Statistics, 2014.

5. Bureau of Labor Statistics, 2014.

PART 2

What We Can Do

CHAPTER TEN

In Search of a New Paradigm

The Effects of the Age Penalty on the 3-C Paradigm

The primary problem with the problematic demographic penalties described in this book—the unrealized income, unfulfilled expenditures, and unrealized tax payments—is that the nation was, and still is, unaware of them. The average individual made less money and will continue to make less for many years, and, consequently, will consume fewer goods and services. Those producers, who realize that the decrease in demand will continue for some time, will begin to supply less and will require less labor will survive. The U.S. workforce represents the largest group of consumers—the employees of all the producers, distributors, traders, investors, and money managers—will suffer as a result. Some will lose jobs; others will lose hours and benefits; and those who do not, at the very least, will work harder without additional compensation. As the typical anxiety and weariness that pervade a culture in recession resumes, demand will decrease again, which brings us back to the beginning of this vicious circle. Like a chain of dominoes, the impact of each financial blow causes the impact of the next and so on until every element of our economy has fallen or, at the very least, felt the hit by growing slower over a very long period of time.

The organizations that will feel these unrealized losses most keenly are undoubtedly local, state, and federal governments. While the average American plans by days, weeks, maybe a few months in advance at most, and the average business leader thinks a fiscal quarter at a time into the future, governments think a minimum of six months to a year at a time and sometimes plan as far as far as the next election cycle, four years into the future. As a result, the demographic penalty on taxes paid makes our current and proposed fiscal policies and actions obsolete and unsustainable. Our elected leaders do not seem to adequately acknowledge the role of the American people in the economy. They do not recognize that the Information Age and globalization have led to a new paradigm where the consumer is king. Our leaders and their advisers are still holding on to the outmoded perception that the chief architects of economic change are their policies and initiatives and business leaders. They seem to operate under the assumption that if American businesses were provided with the right policies and strategies, they would eliminate obstacles and regulations, alter course when necessary, and lead us onward to prosperity.

To put this idea in the norms of macroeconomics, our leaders believe that they can stimulate economic growth by increasing the value of the variables of the classic expenditures formula for calculating the GDP: $Y = C + I + G + (X - M)$. More specifically, the prevailing wisdom is that if we increase government spending (G) or enlarge the amount of currency available by lowering interest rates (in some cases to zero), and provide a direct line of credit from the taxpayers' pockets to those who can qualify in America, then this would increase investment (I) in production, which in turn would increase consumption and, therefore, GDP. Is it incorrect to think that in the international market place, imports and exports can be counted on to augment any shortfalls; that the world is experiencing the same demographic transformation. This method is elegant in its simplicity and applies the type of common sense that we admire so much in America. But it is fraying at the edges.

Although the method is logical, uses quantitative data, and is even supported by an equation, the answer is wrong. As we learned from attempts to stimulate the economy in this manner over the past seven years, this is perfect example of the "labor gap" discussed earlier and a perfect illustration of Steven Levitt's observation that when it comes to economics the "conventional wisdom is often wrong."[1] This pattern of thinking that has become increasingly common and can be characterized as the 3-C economy: we can control the economy through a set of actions taken by a centralizing and controlling set of actors that provide the right amount of capital. In conjunction with this view, our elected officials also assume that they can correct any trade imbalances by either modifying the trade agreements or developing strategies to control trade balance surpluses or adjust exchange rates. Similarly, if any public good is wanting in our society, then the government will simply establish a program or put a control in place to solve it. Generally, the underlying assumption of the 3-C model is that public officials can create fiscal policies and regulations inside the Beltway to control the economy outside it. We have become so dependent on this approach that we have come to expect our political and economic policies to provide for us.

The result of this way of thinking is the perplexing economy of today. Our 3-C paradigm is beginning to shudder and even stall. These approaches are not working, and future political changes that are currently on the policy table during the 2016 political cycle will most likely make it worse. This approach may be necessary at times, but the tools our government has at its disposal are not sufficient to deal with the changes that are occurring, particularly the demographic transformation that is underway throughout the world, with its many causes. I have used the rapid retirement of baby boomers without a sufficient working-age population to replace them as a convenient way of introducing the subject. The question is what do we do about it?

As noted in Chapter 2, the globalization of trade and the advent of Internet technology changed how the economy operates and who is in charge. In the past, reliance on our business and governmental leaders seemed to suffice. There were periods of great uncertainty and at times downright failures; but, through thick and thin, we turned to business and government leaders for results. The advent of consumers armed with a World Wide Web of information and price comparisons, consumer reports, inventory and logistic management, and locations of nearest distributors, combined with a global supply system, granted every one of us as much power as the head buyers of the largest and most powerful corporations of 30 years ago. We had information that used to take executives much of their careers shaking hands and exchanging favors to obtain and a global supply system of unprecedented efficacy. Since the first decade of the new millennium, citizens of most democratic countries can buy any product they can afford, made anywhere in the world, whenever, and have it delivered by hand to their front door in usually a couple of days. No longer do we rely on the old hierarchies when producers were unapproachable, only friends who worked in the same industry had access to wholesale distributors, and most everyone shopped retail. Trade in products, services, and information were liberated from the old fortresses of power, and this old economic paradigm that had reigned for the past two centuries began to change. For the first time in American history, a power worthy of the utopian ideal the framers of our Constitution imagined for the people seemed to be coming true: the promise of a life in which each individual held fundamentally the same rights: the freedom to "life, liberty, and the pursuit of happiness." We did not start with the same opportunities or money, but we had access to the same information, the same prices, and the same distributors. Now, we have the authority and agency to make our own economic decisions. We have become suspicious of insider information particularly by political leaders. For the past decade and a half, we have had access to multiple products made all over the world at our fingertips. The advent of the logistically supported supply chain has changed the cost structure of this centrally controlled system.

Business is adjusting to this shift by becoming focused on customer satisfaction with their products and services, as evidenced by the immediate requests for comments, ratings, and review. Governments are encountering more complicated challenges as they respond to this paradigm shift with individuals as the dominant economic actor. The strategies that we relied on in the past to get individuals to pay sufficient taxes to cover the minimum of public goods we need to keep our society functioning are beginning to break down, for several reasons. First, the demographic penalties of incomes and consumption are not growing as rapidly as the demographic penalty of taxes paid which is almost a 50 percent growth rate reduction that started since the millennium. The movement toward a more conservative view of government and a policy of not increasing taxes has a sound economic driver behind it. The demographic penalty for taxes paid by individuals is reducing our general source of revenue, leaving us to make the difficult decision of whether to spend our money, which is also declining, on public goods or market goods. Government has not adjusted to this changing reality by either improving services or marketing them better, or developing new ways of paying for them. Where is the PayPal of government? Where is the right-sizing of government and the evolution of governance to do things differently in government?

Coinciding with this change is the liberation, empowerment, or sense of authority that women have over their bodies, their reproduction cycle, and the number of children that are brought into the world. As previously noted, this change in the fertility rate is a worldwide phenomenon. It is the most fundamental and influential force in the demographic cycle. Simultaneously, changes in medicine, food production, revolutionary global food distribution systems, and massive infrastructure improvements in water, energy, and other amenities have extended our lives. We learned from previous chapters that collective individual choices have significant impacts on our economy and revenues used to support our government. Decisions on fertility rates and our ability to prolong life are individually generated, but the impacts are collective.

What was once thought to be rather predictable social science, demographics, is shifting and changing. Forces and dynamics discussed in previous chapters have accelerated changes in the demographic cycle. The global era in which goods and services move quickly and easily cross borders, and where information and money moves even quicker and easier, also created an environment that increases the likelihood that individuals would move from their country of origin. This has accelerated the immigration rate and is creating a new social tension between globalization and national cultures and values. The area of demographic analysis that historically has been most uncertain, immigration, is now being joined by rapid changes in birth and death rates. In conclusion, when demographic change is added to the mix, transformations of our population in terms of births, aging, labor patterns, unemployment, and retirements occur rapidly in society today. It is no wonder that our economy is perplexing and our politics are confounding.

Moving from a 3-C to a 3-D Paradigm

The confluence of these major changes in trade, information, and demographics are altering the role of the individual within society and within the economic system. We are entering what Thomas Kuhn called a "the model shift" in the way our economic and political system operates.[2] The process of hierarchy and control of business and government over the economy, which has evolved over the past decades, is now being altered by these changing forces, marking the development of a new paradigm. The impacts are hard to recognize but are of a sufficient size that when we do begin to understand them, nobody knows what to do about them. As Kuhn notes, we are entering a period of a "paradigm shift" that is sudden, profound, and transformative.

At the center of this shift is the increasing role that individuals are performing. This shift can be characterized as *decentralized*, with individuals and not firms or nation-states being the driver; *diversified*/fragmented with multiple products (market goods) and strategies (public goods) coming from multiple places and integrated; and *distributive*, linking individuals more closely to products, services, and strategies with new ways of paying directly for them, which is facilitated by the Information Age technology— forming a new paradigm described as 3-D. This is not a Hollywood technology, but rather an exciting new way of seeing the world. A new paradigm is beginning to evolve that is modifying the path of economic decision making for all goods and services, public and market. So, what path do we take to make further progress?

Before moving to that question, we should also briefly look at the most disturbing of all the transformations occurring globally—that is, the way war is evolving. Rather than acts of aggression initiated by governments and organizations for the purpose of war, acts of terror are initiated by more diffuse entities through destructive choices made by individuals and diversified organizational structures. Terrorism needs to be included in how we look at the way we address our economic transformation for several reasons. Most profoundly, terrorist acts are driven by individual choice

and actions in an information-supported environment. These transformations all require the national policy-making apparatus to operate differently
and will have powerful impacts on our economic and political system.

How we are dealing with this paradigm shift? We only have to look at the
political dialogue in the country, punctuated by election rhetoric, to understand that no one has a clue what to do about this. Easy answers like "We
have to rely on government policies, programs, and actions to fix the problem," or "Just get government out of the way and the market will solve the
problem" is what we have heard during the past decade in the political arena.
The polarized and contentious political dialogue does not go much beyond
these platitudes. When it does, solutions are proposed that will make the
harmful effects of the current transformation even more difficult to solve.
We spent years listening to people misdiagnose the problem with much finger pointing. Resolution or redefining the paradigm will require collective
policies; namely, *our federal system of government will need to engage individuals
differently.* Not an easy task to think about or to suggest a new pathway.

New Rules of the Game for a New Paradigm

Guidance can be found in the Nobel Prize work of Douglass C. North
on institutional design and economic performance. Institutional design is,
in brief, a set of principles established by policy makers that change the
formal rules of the game for society by enabling all of the organizations—
public, private, and nonprofit—within it to function and achieve their
goals. Institutional design provides formal rules for integrating divergent
politics and various public policies together while recognizing that informal forces—cultural, historical, and personal—must be considered to
achieve new economic objectives.[3] While proposed as an approach for
developing economies, North's work suggests a new path to explore for our
highly developed economy that is beginning to sputter. Which raises the
question: can we shift from a 3-C to a 3-D paradigm and alter the looming
long-term decline in our GDP growth rate?

As a starting point, the demographic characteristics of the population
as an informal constraint need to be explicitly identified and considered
in the decision-making process. Providing information and understanding
to the political process is essential if new rules of the game are to generate
formal rules for all the actors to move to a different place. North suggests
that we consider the previously omitted social science information into our
economic assumptions. He also looks to the choice world of politics and
political science as a way of changing a static set of economic considerations.
For North, changing institutions and institutional design, the rules of the
game, alter how organizations work together and transform a path that is

not working into one that could provide a new formula for economic development.

North's work was primarily aimed at finding a solution for developing countries, but it could just as easily be useful for even the most advanced economy in the world. Institutional design for North is a new form of productivity achieved through new rules of the game that guide how the organizations in a society work together to change a path of economic growth that is not working, which can be added to technology in order to increase the performance of labor and, ultimately, the economy. Consider the way we organize ourselves collectively: if we could alter the role of the individual, then we could alter the performance of the economy; if we change the way the sectors—public, private and nonprofit—in our society work together, we alter the performance of our economy; if we change the way the different levels of government work together from the hierarchical top down 3-C to a partnership 3-D relationship, we change the performance of the economy. North's methodology offers a vehicle to practically understand how we could apply the collective power of individual choice to our economy. The most basic of all decisions to regenerate ourselves and to take care of our lives should be integrated with our public choices in the political process that engage with the economic world. Another way of expressing what this is all about is to consider how to establish and manage the interconnections between people and money, resources, and the political process. It is also plausible to think that what we are witnessing in the current political process is nothing more than the beginning of the move from a 3-C to a 3-D paradigm. Carrying out a change in the way our society and our culture works will require fundamental change in the rules of the game in our democratic world. As we are now experiencing, this could prove to be a very difficult period ahead of us.

Understanding the Collective Power of Individual Choice

The first step is to understand the change in assumptions implied by demographics. More than just births, deaths, and migrations, demographics is about the personal decisions involved in creating human culture and civilization in the world around us. Spending time reflecting on our assumptions is not something we like to do or something we are even accustomed doing. Assumptions are sometimes footnotes, briefly mentioned or sometimes even ignored. We are people focused on the bottom line who want 60-second answers and conclusions. For several reasons, this approach will need to change if we want to change course.

First, the demographic penalties that have been identified and quantified not only need to be considered as assumptions but also made an integral part of our analysis. If the collective power of individual choice can have the cumulative effect of taking a substantial portion of income growth out of the economy or almost halving the growth rate in the amount of taxes that people pay to all levels of government, then we need to understand, discuss, and thoroughly know the implications for both the short and long run. In addition, we need to develop a strategy for how we change the way organizations in our society work together. What formal rules can we develop to accomplish this new path requires we change our assumptions and our outlook?

To understand how individual choice becomes a collective choice, we need to look at the world of collective thinking, or systems thinking. Over the past several decades, there has been a proliferation of analytical models that help us think this way. Even more helpful is the development of the world of big data, which will enable us to improve upon these tools. The following is a discussion of the models that are in use today. They include the demographic insights, presented in earlier chapters, in ongoing decision making throughout the country.

To make these determinations, it will be necessary to convert the age elasticities of income, consumption, and taxes paid that can be calculated from the annual Consumer Expenditure Surveys into economic implications useful to decision makers throughout the economic system, particularly ourselves. The analysis in this book is based on sensitivity runs, and the results are presented in Chapters 3–5. Decision makers in the economic system will benefit by knowing what these changes will be in the entire economic system on an on-going basis. Using the tools that are now employed at the national level forecast the economic impacts of our national budget is a good starting point. These forecasts are used to evaluate the national budget, national tax policy and national legislative issues. The Congressional Budget Office has developed a long-term model for the country. I use the model developed by the Congressional Budget Office because it uses a demographic database of long-term growth as a starting point. The analysis is used by both political parties in evaluating legislative proposals and enjoys a degree of trust and confidence. One of the more visible uses of the model is the long-term forecast of the deficit described in Chapter 6. The CBO analysis points to our debt, which is primarily the result of the cost of health and pensions caused by the rapid aging process of our population. These programs are not sufficiently covered by existing funding sources. Additionally, it is not clear that the resulting demographic age penalty has been included in any of the estimates of long-run revenues; thus, it is possible that the increasing debt calculations could be even larger.

As discussed earlier, the changing performance of the economy and the negative impact on the tax revenues associated with the demographic penalties may not be discussed in the CBO work. Furthermore, there is no public discussion of the model itself or any of the assumptions of the model. Congress is not provided this information, with the explanation that the objective results of the model are controversial; by keeping the model operation, content, and assumptions hidden, the modeling and data don't become an issue. The political debate is focused on the results of the analysis. Essentially, the political process in federal decision making is relying on a black box. Objective reality is maintained by including both parties in the staff selection process and by relying on objective reporting and the staff's reputation. This approach may be well and good in the worsening fractious politics of today, but if we want to move past the current dysfunctional dialogue in the country, transparency, openness, and public understanding is an essential starting point. In contrast, the CBO model and assumptions are not transparent and not explained. Efforts are underway to develop open source modeling processes that will conduct third party analysis and supply independent and transparent model results.[4] This work could provide a vehicle for discussing assumptions, including those discussed in this book.

While a third party approach could provide a vehicle for conducting the analysis, it does not solve the larger problem of finding a way to make this information part of the public dialogue. People need to know the collective implications of their individual decisions and the economic implications of both the revenue as well as expenditure implication of demographic change. The new decision makers are individuals collectively making market decisions, reproductive decisions, and political decisions. They must have a full understanding of the economic consequences of these demographic decisions. Lack of transparency leaves individual decision makers in the dark about events that will influence their decisions. Since many of these choices will be made outside of the Beltway, it is only logical that Washington, D.C., makes its analytical capacity available to the people whose lives it will most affect.

The 3-D paradigm shift that is evolving in states, economic regions, and local governments will have similar needs. It is imperative that people know how their decisions will affect the national economy. Better-informed individuals are better equipped to make decisions that will determine the fate of their country. If there is not the same discussion and understanding of assumptions and analysis, the country will be going in multiple directions. Unfortunately, as we saw in Chapter 6, there is little discussion about long-term economic thinking and budgeting at all levels of government. The Government Accountability Office in the *Annual Fiscal Report on State and Local Governments* is the main source of that analysis today. The model used to conduct this work employs long-term demographics to assess the increasing costs that local governments will face. But it does not include an analysis of the impacts of the age penalties on the economy and the revenue sources of government. So, we have two constraints that will need to be overcome: first, learning to look at the long term, economically and fiscally; and, second, learning to include demographic implications in this work. The GAO is currently exploring adding the demographic changes to their framework. It is also exploring how to disaggregate their work to be more helpful to states and local governments.

Other forums for including demographic thinking in the analysis include educational and business forecasting organizations throughout the country. These efforts have the advantage of including more specific data that is particular to their geographic location. While not specifically discussed in previous chapters, demographic penalties were developed for the state of California, the economic region of Southern California, and for the city of Los Angeles. As expected, there was variation among the three geographies. The state had penalties that were less than Southern California's, due to the high economic performance of the Bay Area economy. Southern California's performance was equivalent to the rest of the nation, and, surprisingly, the city of Los Angeles was actually lower than the nation.

As previously noted, analysis does not lead to understanding and action unless it is useful to those who are making decisions. Economic information about our 3-C economy today has been effectively transferred to the decision makers, private and public, inside the Beltway and to businesses in a variety of ways. Philip Tetlock, a professor at the Wharton School of Business who studies forecasting, looked at 28,000 forecasts over 20 years and concluded that chance was almost as accurate as the forecast. The best sources of information are road-testing ideas and the observations of customers.[5] In the future, economic information, including the information about how we affect the economy, will need to be shared with all parties. Suggestions on how to do this will be shared in following chapters.

Notes

1. Steven Levitt and Stephen J. Dubner, *Freakonomics* (New York: Harper Perennial, 2003).

2. Thomas Kuhn, *The Structure of Scientific Revolutions: 50th Anniversary Edition* (Chicago: University of Chicago Press, 2012).

3. Douglass C. North, *Institutions, Institutional Change and Economic Performance* (New York: Cambridge University Press, 1991).

4. "Cracking Washington's Black Box," *Wall Street Journal*, April 4, 2016, p. A18, https://www.google.com/search?q="Cracking+Washington's+Black+Box%2C+Review+and+Outlook%2C+Wall+Street+Journal%2C+April+4%2C+2016.

5. Rachel Emma Silverman, Joann S. Lublin, and Rachel Feintzeig, "CEOs Put Less Stock in Predictions," *Wall Street Journal*, July 13, 2016.

CHAPTER ELEVEN

The New Rules of the Game for a New Pathway

Why Our Current Path Is Unsustainable

The big picture, painted by numbers, of national, state, and local levels of analysis helps us to understand the collective dimension of the transition that we are experiencing. But it is only a start. Most understanding comes from experience, and the experience of this change will be difficult and painful for the nation.

Just how painful it will be is revealed in the declining national growth rate over the past 15 years. That followed 30 years of increases in GDP, which grew, on average, 3.9 percent each year from 1969 to 2000 but plummeted to 1.8 percent per year on average from 2001 to the present. Granted, we had the great recession, but there were a number of recessions in the three-decade period prior to the millennial. Personal income grew in the same time period on average 3.8 percent each year from 1969 to 2000 and fell to 1.8 percent on average per year from 2001 to present. Personal consumption had very similar growth rates, rising 3.4 percent on average per year, and then falling to 2.1 percent on average per year. The most disturbing and most visible difficulty is the fiscal stress of government. Taxes paid by individuals grew 3.8 percent on average each year in the three decades prior to the millennium but dropped to 1.7 percent on average per year since then.[1] These changes in our economic behavior have rattled the nerves of the country, turned the political process upside down, and resulted in difficulty and hardship for a majority of Americans. The demographic changes in the age structure have quietly and unknowingly been a cause, if not the major factor, in this declining economic performance.

Previous chapter showed that changes in "We the People" have collectively resulted in hidden penalties for the past 15 years: $3.34 trillion of unrealized GDP—$238.7 billion per year; $2.73 trillion of consumption—$182.4 billion per year; and $2.27 trillion of unrealized taxes—$132.7 billion per year. Of additional concern, the demographic penalty begins to accelerate at a far greater rate in the decades ahead as more people retire and the growth of our working-age population grows but at a far slower rate. Over the next twenty years, the penalties of GDP is a staggering $28.1 trillion–$1,406 billion average per year; income $24.5 trillion–$1,228 billion average per year; and taxes $10.4 trillion–$520 billion average per year. (Constant 2015 dollars). The only conclusion that can be drawn from this picture is that demographics change is having a profound impact on the economy, and this negative impact will only increase. Furthermore, this impact is causing an unraveling in America politically and socially.

Neal Gabler put a human face on what this means in his article "My Secret Shame" in the *Atlantic Monthly*,[3] writing that "47 percent of Americans [including himself] would not be able to come up with $400 for an emergency . . . without selling something or borrowing or not meeting the emergency." He concluded that a sizable number of Americans are sliding into financial impotence and realizing that they need to take control of their financial lives. Through it all, there is the faint feeling that technology will conquer all and provide the solution. But over the same period, productivity growth over the past 15 years has fared even worse, growing at 1.1 percent per year, and it is not forecasted to grow much faster in the decades ahead.

What Could Be Our Response? Changes in Our Informal Rules

It is often said that Americans will only respond to a crisis. Can painting a picture by numbers, no matter how good the analysis is, establish a defining moment that crystalizes a crisis? Not likely. History provides us an example of a clarion call highlighting the effect of the upcoming demographic transformation that was unheeded. The Committee for Economic Development of the Conference Board published a report *Demographic Change and the American Future* by Scott Fosler, William Alonso, Jack A Meyer and Rosemary Kern in 1990 that clearly identified that the United States would have a positive impact on its economy from an increase in the working age population in the decade of the 1990's and urged to country to capitalize on this advantage to prepare for the challenges of the next century with increasing elderly populations and a decrease of working age population.[4]

So what to do when the underlying forces causing the gradual slow decline occur in a rapidly transforming world? What we are facing is not a business cycle downturn that will cause a crash and a crisis, but a gradual deterioration with some cyclical changes encountered along the way. What we are experiencing is likely to be far more difficult to cope with and will not turn around unless something is done. How do we change a path that is not working?

When facing a tough, long challenge you don't rely on the rush of adrenalin of a crisis to help you respond. Rather, as Douglass North writes, you rely on your inner core strength and wisdom to develop a path that overcomes limitations and moves you toward your goals. What are the core strengths of America? This is a question with many answers. We are blessed with many natural and physical resources, a desirable location, and our system of government with our federal democratic structure, and the character and behavior of American people. While all are important and all contribute to the grand experiment that is America, the two that are important to North's insights are governmental structure—formal rules, and the makeup and behavior of the population. These are our core strengths, and both are essential for a new pathway or strategy to be forged.

There is a long history of the evolution of governance structures to achieve economic objectives in America. Most notable, Nathan Rosenberg and L. E. Birdzell Jr., in *How the West Grew Rich*, provide an insightful history of how Western countries transformed into wealth-generating countries not because of corporations and mass production but because they developed political systems that were flexible and diversified.[5] Over time, these countries broke down centralized political and religious control. They created an environment that fostered the reciprocal dynamics among science, technology, and the marketplace. Their decentralized economic organization allowed multiple diverse enterprises to emerge with authority to make decisions about introducing innovation, hiring the means of production, engaging in markets, and reaping the financial reward for their risk.

The United States went even further in this Western world evolution by experimenting at the local and community levels, as chronicled by Alexis de Tocqueville. He described the decentralization of experimentation that occurred in the evolution of democratic governance in America.[6] De Tocqueville marveled at the ability of Americans to work through associations to achieve common public objectives. Key to the development of the country was Americans' positive attitude and willingness of to work together in building not only their individual farms and enterprises but also their common amenities. America's democratic experiment fostered an economic environment that was unrivaled for centuries until the recent ascendency of China and its modern miracle.

Jane Jacobs in *Cities and the Wealth of Nations* further elaborates on the wealth-creating role that cities, operating through economic regions, can perform through import substitution strategies that generate economic growth.[7] Cities operating within their economic regions provide growth, wealth, and the funding to advance the needs of all the inhabitants of the region. Jacobs focuses on the dynamics of cities. They build the amenities to improve the quality of life. They also build through their economic regions a network of new cost-effective opportunities to provide their economic needs. Successful city-regions built wealth by satisfying more of their needs, hence import substitution, using the resources from this enterprise to further enhance economic development in the city-region. By focusing on enhancing the economic growth of the city-region through strategies that increase what consumers' purchase, the path of economic development is altered.

The challenge of developing a new pathway is built into our DNA. How we started and grew as a nation was built on a solid foundation. All the organizations in our society contributed to the well-being of individuals in society. The common element in this history is decentralized action that is diverse and flexible. It allows and incentivizes individuals while, at the same time, providing for the good of the whole. This brief history suggests that the culture and values of America are very comfortable in the 3-D space of decentralized, diversified, and distributed economic activity. The creativity of America is enhanced when highly flexible, reciprocal, and complex interactions are allowed to flourish. Moreover, if these interactions are encouraged by the dynamics of regional synergy, as suggested by Jacobs, they could expand economic activity. Finally and most important, individual dreams, initiative, and accountability are the foundation of our early history. Government has been sought out to assist us collectively to fulfill these dreams. So we have much to build on.

John H. Cochrane, in a *Wall Street Journal* Opinion piece, discusses the World Bank's ranking of nations on the ease of doing business, including local construction and building permits, paying taxes, moving commerce around the country, and protecting property rights. The ranking on per capita income is against the World Bank's "Distance to Frontier" ideal of 100 percent. Of the 189 countries, the United States was ranked at

90 percent in meeting the criteria and is among the top countries in the world.[8] The World Bank's assessment shows that while we have benefited from historical economic development decisions, there is room for improvement. Of note, this ranking is derived from the perspective of the producer and government, not from the evolving role of the consumer, the new decision maker. As we craft a strategy to deal with the demographic penalties of the next several decades, the tipping point for success will be redefining how business and government enhance the ability of individuals to make collective choice decisions that will enhance economic growth.

Chronicling the Change in America

Reading contemporary writing about how well we are doing in this redefining process is interesting, revealing, and instructive. Our national political battles are not conducive to generating ideas or actions that could be helpful. Rather, local and regional stories and experiments are where we are likely to find examples for defining our new pathway. Not surprisingly, experimentation historically was generated locally and not nationally; witness where de Tocqueville travelled to find his insights on American democracy. Experimentation at the local and regional levels is again being chronicled. These stories serve as guideposts for developing formal and informal rules of the game that will enable public, private, and nonprofit organizations to break out of the undesirable growth patterns facing the nation.

James Fallows and his wife Deborah Fallows traveled the country in a small plane for three years. Updating de Tocqueville's work, they describe how San Bernardino, California; Bend, Oregon; Duluth, Minnesota, Greenville, South Carolina; Pittsburgh, Pennsylvania; Detroit, Michigan; Eastport, Maine; and scores of other places are experimenting with "laboratories of democracy." They identify 11 elements that will mark the regeneration of America, including divisive national politics seem a distant concern; public-private partnerships are real; they have unusual schools; they have big plans; they have and care about a community colleges; and they know about the civic story. An interesting side story is about the role of libraries in furthering technology, education, and community.[9]

Reading through the stories, you find new businesses that are evolving and new industries that are hiring large numbers of people. For example, ESRI, a company founded by Jack Dangermond, is located in Redlands, California, where he prefers to live. Dangermond's company does geographical information system (GIS) mapping. The company is a pioneer in big data, which is quickly transforming how we understand our complex world. It employs 10,000 people worldwide with 2,500 in Redlands, a neighbor of San Bernardino. The firm is located in a small community with a much lower cost structure than the larger city in the region, Los Angeles, and it has an attractive regenerated downtown. The employees have access to regional airports (Ontario is nearby), the research facilities of University of California at Riverside are almost adjacent, and the region has cultural and natural amenities. Most important, GIS and big data are foundational resources that enable individual decision makers to make sense of the world they live in on a daily basis. This story epitomizes what Jacobs wrote about 30 years ago. It shows the power of innovation and small-town thinking in an economic region. GIS was developed as a tool to further the use of parks and recreational activity in the area. The product and service was extensively used and consumed within the region and is now exported to the world. It is not coincidental that this story is about an industry that exemplifies the most important transformation occurring in the country and the world. It is enabling individuals to be the decision makers by making large data and information mapping accessible to everyone.

Building Mega-Regions: The New Global Building Block

Are the Fallows' stories merely interesting or the beginning of a new narrative? You be the judge! Their essay documents the spirit of cooperation, innovation, and enterprise in an America that is alive and well. It exists in every region in the country—not a bad foundation for a broad-scale economic regeneration.

Another story that reinforces the existence of a new emerging paradigm is Michael Storper's *The Rise and Fall of Urban Economies: Lessons from San Francisco and Los Angeles.*[10] The book describes how the Bay Area created and grew the "new economy." It is becoming the most dominant economic region in the country, and the world, in terms of its value added to the nation and the world and the cradle of the third century industrial revolution. The region also has the highest per capita income in the nation. But the region, like all growing regions in the country, is now facing the problems of success: high housing costs, increasing income inequality, and ongoing issues associated with growth and development. The evolution of the Bay Area helps explain the economic paradigm shift that is occurring in the country and helps chart a new pathway for economic development.

The Bay Area has played a key role in the evolution of the new Information Age economy, which is redefining how individuals participate in economic and social structures. Silicon Valley and the Bay Area are the birthplace of technologies that allow individuals/consumers to become something more: the decision makers of tomorrow.

The insights from Storper's book provide a platform for moving the economic base of the country. The transformations that are occurring challenge static assumptions about how organizations behave and relate to one another that makes them less productive and less open to change. Additionally, the complexity and rigidity of current reciprocal relationships between and among sectors in our society further frustrate interactions. In particular, suspicion and lack of trust between the public and private sectors stymies progress. Finally, the existence of large organizations operating within a region, either public or private can preclude cooperative working relationships from developing. A core finding is that organizations, working through networks in a regional context, are more important than ever before. Complexity in relationships and context demand increased reciprocity among technology (innovation, finance, and deployment), production, marketing, and distribution. Finally, interaction among the leaders of organizations in the region must understand the marketplace, which is now driven by decision-making consumers and requires feedback loops with the marketplace. The Bay Area success is in identifying and creating this pathway. Most interesting is that this discovery took place in the halls of industry led by an emerging new group of "captains of industry."

The role of Sand Hill Road, chronicled in the Storper book, illustrates how this new form of interaction evolved. This road travels from west of Stanford University, where the new captains live; along a tract of new commercial office buildings that houses the largest concentration of venture capital firms in the nation; along the boundary of Sanford University that is home to both scientific and business faculty of the inventive class; and continues east toward the San Francisco Bay to the incubators, marketing firms, and companies that generated the products of the new industries. This is just one of many such roads in the region that are built around the multiple research universities located within close proximity of one another including, in addition to Stanford, the University of California–Berkeley across the bay; the University of Santa Clara and San Jose State University, both south down the 101 and the El Camino Real. There are multiple roads and complexes through the region, some across the bay emerging around the University of California in Berkeley, some near Sacramento to the east around the University of California at Davis, Sacramento State, the University of the Pacific, and more.

Why here? What enabled this economic base change dynamic to occur? Several factors were cited. First and foremost, a culture of both openness and diversity in social, racial, and ethnic factors, art, and politics emerged during the expansive and explosive development of the area in the post-war period. Prior to that time, the region was locked in a closed and isolated set of organizations. Next, there was no large "dog" among political and business organizations. In fact, some of the large business organizations, such as Bank of America, moved away. So organizations felt safer working together. The region specialized in creating associations such as the Bay Area Council that involved the business network throughout the region. Board members of the Bay Area Council populated many of the business enterprises in the growing region and created a forum for the exchange of ideas and interactions. They facilitated multiple "industry clusters." They supported needed infrastructure and public investment and created a "Bay Area first" political mentality. This dynamic propelled the economy of the region. What the Bay Area did was take the energy and vitality that the Fallows found in America at the community and city levels and elevated it to a regional level, creating a critical mass that made a difference in changing the region's economic pathway.

What evolved was not a large center city with one large industry that drove the creation of a new economic base, but rather a horizontal region with pockets of diverse, complex, reciprocal relationships that were knitted together by business organizations with political and social values of "inclusiveness, diversity and collaboration," the mission statement of a Bay Area organization called California Leadership.[11]

These are the informal rules of North's theory of economic growth. These values were embedded in the way that leaders and the workforce of these organizations thought and worked. This cooperative value system, along with the quality of life in the Bay Area, attracted entrepreneurial and inventive business leaders to relocate. Workers moved from firm to firm in much the same way that ideas and money did, creating a more mobile and flexible workforce. The formal rules were legislative initiatives that put these principles into societal objectives—for example, protecting minority interests (racial and ethnic inclusion and gender equality), public/private partnerships and new forms of governments, B corporations (public benefit corporations), and other institutional arrangements to deal with the issues of the greater region, such as bay protection, coastal protection, transportation, and housing.

The informal principles of flexible collaboration, inclusiveness of parties, and diversity of actors and participants in the decision-making process are creating a new economic base. These principles are providing the resources to regenerate and grow the region and communities throughout the state. They also help address the quality-of-life and cost-of-living issues that could undermine the growth. It should be noted that the success of creating a new economic base could be undermined if there is not a simultaneous regeneration of the public sphere in the region.

Public Sector Leadership Principles for the New Economy

The public sphere is undergoing a similar transformation. Based on the same informal rules but translated into a formal rule enacted by the legislature at the request of California governor Jerry Brown, this legislation evolved out of the regions' search for an instrument to fund infrastructure while achieving other objectives. These provisions, called enhanced infrastructure districts and public finance authorities (PFAs), are based on the informal values discussed earlier.[12] Cities and counties create districts based on investment plans that address the economic development, infrastructure, and environmental mitigation needed to support the economic, environmental, and equity goals of the district, which could be a community, city, county, or region.

The investment plan must show that those who benefit from the investment will provide the revenues needed to support the investment either through direct usage payments or through capturing part of the increased value generated by land use policies and/or the investments in infrastructure. The districts' PFAs are separate governmental entities. The members of the PFA are any public agency that brings resources to the table and are considered separate public entities. They can be of any size—community, city, county, region, substate—and can easily cross jurisdictional boundaries. Using projected revenue streams from the beneficiaries of the investments to back the securities, with 45-year payback schedules, the instruments are sold on the capital markets. Their mission is to bring multiple funding streams together to complement our tax structure approach, creating sufficient funding streams to address refurbishing and building the infrastructure, investing in economic development, and funding environmental mitigation such as air quality. These entities have the authority to enter into public/private partnerships that bring additional funding to the investment program; and they have all the funding legislative authority in the state code, provided there is a direct relationship between beneficiaries and the expenditure.

For this approach to work, it will require that keen attention be paid to the new decision maker, the user, and land-owning beneficiaries who will directly pay for the investments that benefit the whole of the community. This revenue structure approach directly engages users with the provision of services in what Geoff Mulgan describes as a "the principle of reciprocity."[13] This creates horizontal structures that enable consumers of public goods (users of the services) or land owners whose property will increase in value due either to zoning changes or the provision of infrastructure and community services to be involved in a reciprocal funding agreement. Success depends on gauging needs correctly by government and private partners. These new funding streams amortize securities sold to capital markets. The better the listening process of the collective decisions of the "consumers," the lower the risks. This is another example of the power of "collective individual choices" where the decision makers are the users and landowners in the district and not government staff and elected officials. Linking economic development with housing, infrastructure, and environment mitigation in integrated investment strategies that stand the test of collective payment structures will create a new sense of ownership, community, and control.

This approach integrates the parts of the system in the development process and links this investment plan to the decision makers who will pay the fare. In this paradigm, individuals are not directed by an outside authority or public agency. Rather, individuals are the architects and builders, and individuals will be willing to pay, to contribute. In many respects, this approach, by changing the rules of the game, enables the public space to operate similarly to our market goods. For this paradigm to be successful, the roles of government at all levels will need to change. The relationship of government to those governed (governance) will be altered to the 3-D approach: decentralized, where goals can be set and complexity managed; diverse, allowing integration of strategy to overcome complexity; and distributed, where there is linkage between investments and users and beneficiaries. What is evolving in the Bay Area, and all the regions of California, is a new pathway, a paradigm of how our society works in both the private and public spheres.

While the Bay Area and the other economic regions in California are experimenting with this approach, so are the other economic regions in the country. The America the Fallows chronicle is nationwide. Our large economic regions blend economic strategies with infrastructure networks in natural ecological regions. Americans are organizing to support new economic growth strategies through the formation of megaregions, first chronicled in America 2050's "A Prospectus,"[14] which describes a regeneration of the large urban cores in the nine megaregions which cover the country, including strategies to revitalize neighborhoods and communities in the large regional urban cores and invest in supply chain infrastructure linking the urban core of these regions with the extended rural and exurban marketplace of the megaregion. The megaregions provide a framework for economic competitive strategies needed to grow the economy of America in the changing global world, and address the growing economic and political divide that erupted in the 2016 presidential cycle.

The Southern California Megaregion—whose economy and geography are larger than all but four states, including California—is an example of how these large economic regions are forming new economic foundations for global competitiveness. The region has become the hub for the logistics supply chain of the nation with rail and truck links throughout nation. Supply and distribution centers are located not only in the region but in neighboring states of Nevada and Arizona. The new consumer-based economy is the driving force creating this new industrial framework. The region is a recreational center for the nation and the world, which is also located in the region and in neighboring states with the Las Vegas/Anaheim–Disneyland as the icon. The population of the megaregion is the core base of visitors. The nation and the world enable this base to thrive. Finally, the region, thanks to Hollywood and the digital revolution, is becoming the content capital of the world.[15]

The highly urban cores in each of the nine megaregions that cover the United States provided Hillary Clinton with almost all her electoral votes; the exurban and rural areas all voted for Donald Trump. These megaregions will be successful if the red and blue areas become purple. All the mega-regions cross state lines, and many cover a large number of states. Economic development and infrastructure strategies that employ the insights that Michael Storper identified in the success of the Bay Area (complexity in regional relationships and context; increased reciprocity among innovation, finance, and deployment in technology; production, marketing, and distribution) can propel these megaregions to become the engine for the United States economy. The dynamics of these megaregions—coupled with infrastructure, supply links throughout the larger region and employing the import substitutions strategy of Jane Jacobs (doing and producing more consumer goods and importing less)—provide a road map for economic development success for the now linked parts of these mega-regions. This possibility provides the nation with a strategy to re-create our economic base, particularly for the middle class, which has eroded over the last several decades.

A new pathway for America is emerging that will alter our economic system. It is based on the core strengths of the nation: flexibility to accommodate change in our political system enables our own the problem-solving nature, which are described in later chapters. We are seeing a new economic base evolving that could provide the opportunities needed to grow the American economy.

Notes

1. Bureau of Economic Analysis.

2. These calculations are derived from a sensitivity run of the demographic age model described in Chapter 5 in which the years of the Great Recession, 2007–2009, are removed to adjust for the Great Recession.

3. Neal Gabler, "My Secret Shame," *Atlantic Monthly*, May 2016.

4. Scott Fosler, William Alonso, Jack A. Meyer, and Rosemary Kern, *Demographic Change and the American Future* (Pittsburgh: University of Pittsburg Press 1990), p. 13.

5. Nathan Rosenberg and L. E. Birdzell Jr., *How the West Grew Rich* (New York: Basic Books, 1987), p. 268.

6. Alexander de Tocqueville, *Democracy in America* (New York: Penguin Putnam Books, 2003).

7. Jane Jacobs, *Cities and the Wealth of Nations* (New York: Random House, 1984).

8. John H. Cochrane, "Ending America's Slow-Growth Tailspin," *Wall Street Journal*, May 2, 2016, http://www.wsj.com/articles/ending-americas-slow-growth -tailspin-1462230818.

9. James Fallows with Deborah Fallows, "Can America Put Itself Back Together?" *Atlantic Monthly*, March 2016, pp. 59–72.

10. Michael Storper, Thomas, Kemeny, Naji P. Makarem, and Taner Osman, *The Rise and Fall of Urban Economies: Lessons from San Francisco and Los Angeles* (Palo Alto, CA: Stanford University Press, 2015).

11. State Senators John Vasconcellos, a Democrat, and Becky Morgan, a Republican, both from the Silicon Valley, founded California Leadership. Its mission was to develop the next generation of leaders for California.

12. These are new California statutes SB628 and AB313, enrolled in 2015 and 2016, that local and regional entities are now beginning to use.

13. Geoff Mulgan, *Connexity: How to Live in a Connected World* (Boston: Harvard Business School Press, 1998).

14. Regional Plan Association, *America 2050: A Prospectus* (New York: Author, September 2006).

15. Mark Pisano, Ronald Brummett, Gary Gallegos, and Pria Hidisyan, "The United States of America's Third Century Strategy: Preserving the American Dream," Southern California Association of Governments. September 2005, http:// america2050.org/pdf/socalmegaregion.pdf.

CHAPTER TWELVE

Managing Our Fiscal Commons

Why Is This Problem So Difficult?

Demographic change has its greatest impact on our already-stressed public sector. The political polarization over the past decade underscores the need to change a course that, if unaddressed, will only get worse as time goes on. The fiscal reality, at all levels of government, is significantly affected by both the growth rate of the economy and the effectiveness of our tax structure. We learned from the previous chapters that demographic change since the start of the millennium is negatively affecting them both. Decline in our nation's long-term economic growth, from 3.8 percent prior to the turn of the last century to 1.8 percent since, as well as a decline of 45.8 percent overall in the growth of taxes paid by individuals, have resulted in a general national decline in taxes paid from 3.4 percent to 1.7 percent. Both of these impacts have led to the fiscal stress that we read about in the press and hear about in the political debates.

The budgeting process at all levels of government is faced with a double whammy. First, governments need to find a way to deal with the negative impacts of declining fiscal resources on the provision of public goods and services: health, education, defense, public safety, environment, housing, jails and probation services, voting rights, and so on. Second, and more important, government has the sole responsibility of enacting the policies, statutes, edicts, and directives—the "rules of the game"—that provide order in our society. These formal rules can change our policy course in order to meet our goals and fix those policies that are not working. The dynamics of budgeting decisions and setting the policies, the "rules of the game" for determining how society works, is also accomplished in the political process, as was described by Aaron Wildavsky in 1988 and has been evolving ever since.[1] When fiscal resources are increasing, it is possible for executives and legislators to make incremental trade-offs in resource allocations and still deal with the policy trade-offs when enacting the rules of the game for society. But in this era of shrinking resources and huge increases in entitlements, budget decisions on resource allocations have become tools and tactics in the debate over policy issues.

This is precisely what is happening at all levels of government today, as different offices have taken on new responsibilities for the provision of services, particularly in the allocation of pension and health benefits. Decisions on entitlements dwarf other budget decisions and compromises the bargaining between budgeting and rule changes. At the federal level, interest group politics dominate because of the size of pensions and health care, and the number of people impacted. As a result, deliberations over policy changes that should enable us to govern become stalemated. The same is also true at the state level as states assume more responsibility for the large entitlement programs. When fiscal resources decline, our public institutions become increasingly dysfunctional. We are unable to resolve governance issues, leading to stalemate, or adopt reform initiatives. We see this happening repeatedly in the U.S. Congress and even in state legislatures, and we wonder why our representatives cannot compromise. The litany of blame has cascaded to a resounding pitch.

When the decline in fiscal resources is long-term, the experience of the last 15 years—which has been the case with the influence of demographic changes on the budget cycle—new approaches and political dynamics are needed. Since fiscal decline is likely to last at least through 2035 and perhaps longer, dealing with this long-run issue may be one of the most difficult challenges that we face in contemporary politics. The actual size of entitlements and the ever-increasing size of the fiscal shortfalls, exacerbated by the negative fiscal implications of our ever-present demographic penalties, will be a source of continuing complication and challenge for public officials.

Before looking at strategies to deal with this, it is necessary to dig deeper into the long-term implications of demographic changes beyond those described in Chapter 7. From 2000 to the present, the demographic age penalty of taxes paid by individuals was $137.7 billion annually. Going forward through 2035, 10,000 baby boomers will retire per day, at which point there will be over 35 million Americans retired. To put these numbers into perspective, consider these assumptions: If labor participation rates continue as they have been—and all indications suggest that they will—if fertility rates continue to decline, and if immigration rates face continued political grandstanding and legal restrictions, then the growth of retired senior citizens will be twice the growth of the working-age population in the United States. This change in age structure results in a taxes paid penalty of $268 billion in 2016, $480 billion in 2025, and $856 billion in 2035 (Constant 2015 dollars). To put these unrealized tax revenues in perspective, the amount of taxes not realized in 2016 was 13.5 percent of those that were paid. Over the next 20 years, the compounded sum of all the age tax penalties will be $10.39 trillion. These are financial resources, which would have gone to federal, local and state governments but for the change in the demographic structure of our population. These penalties are greater than half of the current national debt. Due to the changes in age structure, the amount of unrealized taxes paid grows to almost 17 percent the projected taxes paid in 2025 and 20.8 percent of taxes paid in 2035 if we do not change the tax structure or find other ways of funding our public goods.

These penalties are annual amounts that will make the already-difficult issue of government fiscal stress unmanageable unless there is a change in our public sector. These are not dips in revenue that come with business cycle downturns that can be expected to rise with the recovery, nor are they a new norm that government can settle into and use incremental budgeting rules to try to sort out the costs between winners and losers, particularly in light of the distortion effect of the large entitlement resource decisions. Governments, at all levels, are facing a long-term financial challenge different from any other in recent American history. Making the problem even more difficult is the erosion of the declining financial resources cannot actually be seen, which is the unrealized reduction of revenues caused by the changes in age, labor, and retirement numbers. Underlying those changes are the most fundamental changes of all: fertility and mortality rates. Unless this pattern is recognized and until we have a conscious set of public policies and strategies to deal with what "we" are doing to both the economy and to government revenues, this silent erosion will continue.

Most of the country seems to be thinking that this is merely the natural business cycle, the "ups and downs" of the market, and that the monetary and fiscal instruments of government will correct our fiscal deterioration. One possible interpretation of the current political dysfunction in the country is that the American people intuit the need for change; we are looking for it and cannot find it. Our first reaction is to blame the establishment, the system, which was the target of the 2016 presidential campaign. This blame game will continue, given the magnitude and stealth nature of the problem. We are still fixated on the belief that what is important is finding who is at fault because it always has to be someone's fault. Expect this sentiment to continue unless: we first, expose the silent nature of the problem and make it transparent using the insights and recommendations of Chapter 10, and second, we do something about it.

To solve the problem, we must alter our economic path. The public sector must change to a decentralized, diverse, and disaggregated (or 3-D) fiscal decision-making framework, relying on our system of government and the character of the American people. In this chapter, we will look at possible strategies for government that are within the constraints of our democratic system; while, in the next chapter, we will look at strategies we can adopt as individual Americans.

A Common-Pool Resource Approach to Fiscal Management

Insight can be found by examining our physical and natural environment which have also been facing scarcity. Our air, water, and other natural resources have been facing long-term threats. For several decades, scientists and public servants have worked together to develop an evolving set of principles called "environmental sustainability" that requires long-term system thinking about how to control the rates of depletion of these natural resources so that future generations will have the same opportunities as we do. On the financial side, we have learned to examine life-cycle costs including "externalities" (the side effects of industrial or commercial activities). For decades, an extensive education program has been informing the public that resource depletion cannot continue indefinitely. Green strategies are now an important part of the country's production processes, and the culture of the country has been shifting to reflect this. Think about how often *green* appears in the advertising and marketing programs for product and services.

The work of Elinor Ostrom, a Nobel Prize economist, studied how common-pool resources are managed in America and around the world.[2] Ostrom's research teams found that, over time, natural resource systems—forests, rivers, and so on—that are managed well and not overextracted by special interests can be replenished to maintain the resource for future generations. From her work and countless case studies, we can develop a roadmap through the fiscal maze in front of us. A research team from the University of Southern California and the University of San Francisco applied Ostrom's methodology to fiscal sustainability to study how governments in Southern California have dealt with fiscal stress since the Great Recession.[3] These Southern California case studies looked into one of the largest local governments in America, Los Angeles County, then on the verge of default. The county turned itself around and provided many insights supporting the Ostrom roadmap. Another jurisdiction, the city of San

Bernardino, which did go bankrupt, showed that not following these strategies and principles could come at a heavy price.

The elements and findings of these case studies are very similar to fiscal common-pool management. The case studies provided insights into characteristics of leaders, their dynamics, and the context that enables a jurisdiction to succeed or fail when facing intense political and economic challenges. Typically we base our analysis of fiscal stress on the electoral process, the budgeting process, and governmental rules of the game. This does not tell us what works or fails. The common-pool approach focuses instead on the characteristics of success. It looks at what good leaders do and what changes in the context or system are needed.

For Ostrom, successful common pools had eight context variables in common, and the leaders of these systems followed six leadership principles. Key among the context variables is the complex nature of multiple activities all nestled together to enable efficient operations. To meet the needs of complex systems, natural or political, a bundle of organizations and activities need to be considered. There are clear boundaries in both space and time, so that the relationship of the parts is known and the effects over time are understood.

Integration of programs and looking at budgets as a system to achieve goals and needs are the starting points for decision making. Most important, there is no substitute for looking at life-cycle costs over time. Failure to do this in a transparent way invites special interests to over extract in the present, sacrificing the future. The politics and practice of budgeting in the context of decades of growing fiscal resources have now created a political incapacity to acknowledge revenue limitations. Political leaders find it difficult to admit that they cannot meet constituents' needs. There is no substitute for transparency and communication among all the parties to come to the realization that different choices need to be made. The choice process includes participants with different roles and responsibilities from elected policy makers and their professional staff to interest group leaders and the citizens for whom these programs and policies exist. Knowing these roles and how to execute the duties assigned to each enables them to work. If there is a breakdown in any role or if a party is left out, the process falters and often generates an overextraction of expenditures. Current examples of overextraction are public sector pensions predicated on revenue streams that are derived on demographic factors, discussed in this book, that will not hold in the future. The long-term payment of these pension obligations come out of future revenues used for other purposes. Another example is not dealing with maintenance of capital expenditures.

If these wasteful mistakes are allowed to continue, ultimately, the common pool-jurisdiction fails.

Looking at fiscal sustainability as a system of managing our common-pool resources and not just balancing expenditures with revenues creates the capacity to deal with long-term financial stress. The U.S. Congress has established many recent budgeting reforms, starting in 1974 when the CBO was established and a long-term perspective was formally introduced into the decision process of the country. Many of Ostrom's principles are reflected in the working of these reforms, but Congress still needs more reforms, particularly to change the single focus of programs and laws. Unfortunately, other levels of government (i.e., states and local governments) have not adopted these reforms, and there is no national consensus that we should. In the casework done to date, aside from the GAO work on future trends in state and local finance and the CBO role in the federal budget, there has been little recognition of what is lurking on the horizon. Chapter 9 describes an approach to begin to make this issue more transparent, understandable, and important. Over time, as occurred with management of our national resources, a culture of fiscal sustainability can be developed to cope with our fiscal crisis.

State and Local Experimentation

In the meantime, experimentation and innovation are happening at all levels of government. There are also highly visible examples of the early casualties: Detroit, San Bernardino, Stockton, Vallejo, and Puerto Rico. The Lincoln Institute of Land Policy has called fiscal sustainability the "Millennial Issue" and has supported research into preparing local and state governments for the future.[4] One effort will be to "operationalize" the common-pool work into a fiscal sustainability index and a handbook and tool box that can be used by public entities over the ensuing decades to deal with fiscal sustainability.

There are examples of change occurring across the country undertaken by individuals working in their communities and economic regions. The modern age de Tocquevilles, James and Deborah Fallows, flew to cities and towns, as described in Chapter 10; the annual National Civic League's "All American Cities" award; the daily blogs of "Route 55," *Governing* magazine, and countless other sources are chronicling case studies of experimentation and innovation going on across the country. This experimentation is aimed at increasing the productivity of the governance of America and is analogous to the experimentation occurring in the private sector. As previously noted, innovation and problem solving in the American people is a competitive advantage of America. Journalists speak about the experiments in communities, stories we can learn from and transfer to the larger community. The economic regions, some of which are multistate, have their own story to tell, as we saw in Chapter 10. The work of Michael Storper and his associates looks at the major regions of California. America 2050, a national nonprofit, describes what is occurring nationwide and has identified nine megaregions that form the economic and ecological foundation for the United States. All these stories focus on the economic environment and infrastructure. Implicit or explicit, these changes are reweaving the institutional design of America's organizations and developing new rules to work together in a more productive manner. Organizations need not only to grow their economies but also to rebuild their governing structures and revenue base in order to fund the public goods and services necessary to accomplish their goals.

We need to know a few things first in order to describe this path. Stories and anecdotes are the raw material we use to think through change, but we need to put them together in a manner so we can collectively learn.

Increasing Government Revenues

Increasing revenues at all levels of government is another approach that government has been pursuing to augment shortfalls. There were several provisions in the Affordable Healthcare Act, some in the form of penalties and increases on higher incomes. Numerous states have increased gas taxes and some, like California and New York, have imposed taxes on upper incomes. Still others, like Ohio and Kansas, have reduced taxes. All told, these changes did not have much of an impact on the reduction of growth in taxes since 2000. The primary approach, however, is not to focus on changing the tax rates, but rather to reform the tax structure itself. Discussion in Congress and the election process has focused on the perceived need to change both the corporate and individual tax codes. Republicans argue that reducing taxes on businesses will increase growth that will, in turn, lead to an increase in taxes paid. Democrats suggest increasing taxes on the upper-income earners and on businesses to cover the new initiatives they propose to fund existing obligations. Similar discussions are occurring in our state houses and local council chambers.

Several insights from the demographic change analysis in Chapter 8 are worth keeping in mind as government deliberates on these recommendations. The effect of tax cuts in the past, when effective, had the synergy of a "demographic bonus"—that is, a bonus to add stimulus and increase growth. When the stimulus turned to penalty, even though the penalties were just beginning, the impact of tax cuts in the latest round was questionable. The demographic penalty will continue for decades and increase dramatically, so we need to be very careful what we wish for. Tax cuts may further exacerbate another problem that could have adverse consequences on our economy, further increasing debt. Given the size of the age penalty on taxes paid, the size of the debt could become even more unmanageable. Also, when growth in incomes and consumption is declining and likely to decline further, it will be difficult to go to voters, particularly those whose incomes are not growing and who are having difficulties in the consumption marketplace, and ask them to pay more taxes. The demographic penalty of the past 15 years helps explain the increased opposition of voters to tax increases. With these penalties increasing in the future, the headwinds of voter opposition to tax increases are likely to get stiffer. If individual income increases are slowing along with corresponding decreases in the growth of consumption/expenditures, then increasing taxes will raise the question of what is to be sacrificed. This is a difficult political environment for those advocating tax increases. Prioritizing needed public goods such as education, health care, infrastructure, public safety and security, and national defense will become a daunting challenge.

Public Finance Authorities

The challenge for our public sector will be to find approaches that help voters agree to increase expenditures for public goods because they provide more benefits to individuals who will, therefore, be willing to sacrifice some of their income for the purchase of public goods. This is the approach being tried in a California experiment called public finance authorities (PFAs; see Chapter 11). These authorities are based on the informal rules and environmental policies established by government, such as zoning and development.[5] They fund the provision of infrastructure, development, and environmental improvement that increases the value of our communities and provides direct services to individuals and businesses. The essence of the change is to create new governance structures that do not tax individuals, businesses, and property and only later decide how to spend these receipts. Rather, governance structures are established that enable individuals, property owners, and businesses to pay directly for public investments that benefit them. New public entities can be established by cities and counties based on investment plans that provide for economic development, infrastructure, and environmental mitigation needed to support the economic, environmental, and equity goals of the new district (whether community, city, county, or region).

The investment plan must show that those who benefit from the investment will provide the revenues needed to support it either through direct usage payments or through capturing part of the increased value generated by land use policies, and/or the investment. The boards of these districts, which are considered separate governmental entities, are cities and counties that have land use responsibilities, and any public entity (e.g., special district) that brings resources to the table. These authorities can issue securities, with 45-year schedules, to obtain resources from the capital markets to be paid back by the funding streams of those who benefit. Their mission is to bring multiple funding streams together in order to complement our tax structure approach. These entities create sufficient funding streams to address infrastructure needs, invest in economic development, and fund environmental mitigation such as, air quality, within the boundaries of the district. They have the authority to enter into public/private partnership arrangements. They can accept state and federal grants and loans. This can bring additional funding to the investment program, and it has all the legislative authority in the state code for funding that is based on a direct relationship between beneficiaries and the expenditures.

For this approach to work, keen attention will be required to design and build investments that the new decision makers (the users and land-owning beneficiaries) will be willing to pay for. This revenue structure approach directly engages users with the provision of services, in what Geoff Mulgan[6] describes as "the principle of reciprocity." This principle creates horizontal structures and enables consumers of public goods and services or landowners whose properties will increase in value to be involved in a reciprocal decision to directly pay. Success depends on gauging needs correctly by government and private partners. The better the listening to the collective decisions of the "consumers," the lower the risks of failure. This is another example of the importance and power of "collective individual choice," where the individual decision makers are the customers.

The informal principles of flexible collaboration, inclusiveness of parties, diversity of actors, and participants in the decision-making process are creating a new economic base. The success of the new economic base could be undermined if there is not a simultaneous regeneration of the public sphere. What is evolving in the Bay Area region, and all the regions in the state, is a new pathway, a paradigm of how our society can work in both the private and public spheres.

Eighteen other states (e.g., Maryland, Virginia, Texas, and Ohio) have begun to enact similar statutes. The governors and mayors know that if they do not regenerate their infrastructure and deal with their natural environment, they cannot grow their states, communities and their economies. The funding structure of this approach does not force anyone to increase taxes. Rather, it enables those who need and want infrastructure services and environmental improvements (which will lead to enhancement of their financial position) to fund it themselves. Furthermore— and even more important—this approach adds to an economic regeneration strategy that is already developing. Just as regions and communities across the country are rebuilding their economic base (as described in Chapter 10), this funding paradigm will provide the resources to undertake infrastructure improvements, provide new jobs, and increase employment opportunities for everyone, particularly the long-term unemployed.

President elect Trump has made infrastructure an early action initiative. To accelerate and increase the national effort, a "Memo to National Leaders: Creating an Infrastructure Funding Market" has been proposed by the National Academy of Public Administration.[7] This "Memo" is based on using Public Financing Authorities (PFA) to develop new revenue streams that pay for securities issued on the capital market and to pension plans. The federal role in this national initiative is to alter federal participation in the investment programs that are funded by the (PFA) s. Currently federal programs, lands, assets and grants are administered in the current 3-C mode of control, centralized and capital intensive described earlier. The "Memo" outlines a change where federal responsibilities become a partnership with state and local governments in the 3-D world of the (PFA) s. Federal programs and investments become part of the investment programs and participate in the wealth creating and capture process of the (PFA). The Federal Government participates in the financial arrangement through existing credit enhancement programs that are capitalized to support a national regeneration program that will support a higher level of economic growth, and provide jobs, particularly for those who are structurally displaced or find themselves in lower paying jobs.

Changing the rules of the game so that individuals can take control by creating new, flexible, and reciprocal structures that are decentralized is creating a new economic base and a new public space.

Notes

1. Aaron Wildavsky, *The New Politics of the Budgetary Process* (New York: Longman, 1988).

2. Elinor Ostrom, *Governing the Commons: The Evolution of Institutions for Collective Action* (Cambridge: Cambridge University Press, 1990).

3. "Southern California Fiscal Sustainability and Governance Project," report to the John Randolph Haynes and Dora Haynes Foundation, June 2014.

4. George W. McCarthy, "Lincoln Institute CEO Discusses Cities' Challenges to Sustain Solvency," presentation to University of Southern California, Price

School of Policy, March 2015, https://priceschool.usc.edu/lincoln-institute-ceo
-discusses-cities-challenges-to-sustain-solvency/.

5. Mark Pisano, "Innovation in Planning and Funding Infrastructure Renewal: The London Experience." In *Innovation in the Public and Nonprofit Sectors,* edited by Patria de Lancer Julnes and Ed Gibson (New York: Routledge, 2016).

6. Geoff Mulgan, *Connexity* (Boston: Harvard University Press, 1997), p. 14.

7. Mark Pisano and John Bartle, "Infrastructure: Building a New Paradigm for Finance and Governance," in *Memos to National Leaders*, ed. Paul L Posner, Janice R. Lachance, and Tonya T. Neaves (Washington, D.C.: National Academy of Public Administration and George Mason University, 2016), pp. 141–146.

CHAPTER THIRTEEN

No One Is Disposable

America's Competitive Advantage: "We the People"

Earlier chapters describe the American people as one of our greatest competitive advantages. In the last three decades of the last century, the increase in the working-age population and the associated demographic age bonus were major contributors to the dynamic growth of the period. The United States' population distribution, while changing, still has a comparative advantage relative to the rest of the developed world.

But the twin issues, working-age population growth and the aging composition of the workforce, almost overnight, without us even knowing or realizing it, started turning from an asset to a liability. The first year of the millennium, 2001, was the tipping point for a shift from a demographic bonus era to a demographic penalty era. Equally problematic was the emergence of a new force that is creating a new challenge for our economy, the "workers' gap." Caused by declining growth in working-age population, the workers' gap stifles economic growth. The dramatic decline in the fertility rate since the 1980s is a significant drag on America's economic growth. This is a global phenomenon. Japan and Europe, East and West, have a far greater problem; and many of the developing world countries, including China, have an unfavorable age population distribution. It is often said that your greatest asset can quickly become a liability if you do not take care of it. So it is with our population.

Earlier chapters have quantified the impact of this tipping point and proposed a new pathway for dealing with the negative impacts of these long-term changes. These proposals build upon America's two greatest assets: the problem-solving capacity of the American people and our governmental system. This chapter will focus on strategies to increase our working-age population. The previous chapter discussed strategies for altering our other key asset, our governmental system.

This discussion is about the availability of working-age population who can participate in the economy. Putting this issue into perspective, growth in our working-age population during the next three decades is projected to be 55 percent less than the growth of the previous three decades.[1] This will yield only a fraction of the economic growth in the past. We know that the growth of the labor force is important to the growth of the economy. It could account for up two-thirds of the growth of the economy, depending on the workers' skills and use of capital. But the reality that growth of workers cannot occur if there is no growth in working-age population, so simple and basic, seems to have been lost in our public policy debates. Rather, there seems to be a view that, if we just provide capital and up the education ante, workers will be available to support any growth objective we want. Workers' skills and the availability of capital, while important, do not appear to be the fundamental source of the problem. Over the past eight years, the Federal Reserve has provided plenty of capital—some would argue too much. The use of capital to improve technology through innovation, as Robert Gordon and others have observed, is also not the answer. We have made education a national priority over the past decades and are working in our states and communities to improve all our educational institutions, public and private. Our higher educational institutions are the envy of the world. We are educating the world's students as well as our own. Our basic problem is that we are not growing our working-age population.

How could it be? We read constantly that the population of the country is consistently growing. And so it is, primarily because our aging population is living longer. We are adding more people to the retiree ranks: 35 million more retirees will be added to our population count over the next two decades. This is not hard to do. Boomers are retiring at a rate of 10,000 persons a day. The aging population and the number of retirees are growing at almost twice the rate of the growth of the working-age population.[2] The working-age population is not just workers for all the sectors, private, public or nonprofit, but also the innovators, entrepreneurs, executives and managers, doctors, lawyers, government and nonprofit leaders—all the personnel needed to run a society. But when you have less than half the number of working age population available to participate in growing our economy, an economic slowdown is inevitable.

More problematic is that many of those in the working-age population, for multiple reasons, have taken themselves out of the available pool of possible workers. Therefore, the number of people available for work is decreasing. The jobs are there. It is true that we have lost manufacturing jobs to other countries since 2000, but we have made those jobs up and more. What's going on?

Let's look at the data. An overview of the sources of incomes of American shows that 68 percent of Americans received their income from wages and salaries in 2000. Just 15 years later, this number was 63 percent, eight million people less earning money from some form of work. In the same time period, the number of Americans receiving their income from government transfer payments increased from 13 to 17 percent, or eight million people receiving transfer payments as their income.[3] While many of these transfer payments are Social Security retirees, boomers started to retire after 2011, many are recipients of Supplemental Nutrition Assistance Program (SNAP), Medicaid, Temporary Assistance to Needy Families (TANF), and other safety net programs. Enrollments in America's safety net programs have increased in the first 15 years of the century. Over 52 million Americans, 21.3 percent of the nation's population, participated in these means-tested programs each month in 2012. Medicaid was the highest at 15.3 percent, followed by SNAP at 13.4 percent. The growth in SNAP since the Great Recession illustrates the growth in our safety net. Over 44 million of the population were recipients of SNAP in 2015, up from 27.6 million since the Great Recession. More than 25 percent of those in the safety net programs are of working age.[4] While these numbers shows the capacity of the nation to provide assistance in this period of transformation and dislocation, particularly during the Great Recession, the question is, what incentives can be provided for this group to increase their participation in the working-age population?

Now add to this the number of people who are in prison or jail, are school dropouts or unwed mothers, have a disability, and the available pool of personnel to work gets even smaller. A closer look at these categories shows substantial numbers of people, and the numbers are growing. In 2016, the American criminal justice system has more than 2.3 million people locked up in prisons, jails, and detention centers. One out of every 100 adults is imprisoned, which is to 5–10 times larger than other Western countries.[5] There are over 20 million people, mostly of working age, who have felony convictions, making it difficult for them to become employed. Federal and state incarcerations have increased fourfold over the past 10 years.[6] An alarming report notes that the number of adults with criminal records is as large as the number with four-year college degrees.[7] A recent finding in a *New York Times*/CBS News/Kaiser Family poll that 34 percent of all nonworking men ages 25–54 have criminal records.[8]

When all possible explanations for the number of working-age population opting out of even trying to be part of the labor force are summed, Nicholas Eberstadt, in *Men without Work*, calculated that if the ratio of men of working-age, 25–54, to the total population were the same today as in 1965, 9–10 million more people could be working today. If you add to this the number of women who have left even trying to find work since 2000, the number would be even higher.[9] The question is, how do we change this unwillingness to be part of the economic system?

This question begs a discussion that is not just about the nagging problem of structural unemployment, which includes workers who find their skills do not fit the current job market and are therefore not able to gain employment for long and sometimes indefinite periods. The transformations occurring in our economy have caused structural unemployment to be persistently high since the Great Recession. Nor is the discussion about frictional and cyclical unemployment, the temporary adjustments that occur during business cycles. These are issues that we pay constant attention to and have multiple strategies and programs to address. We need to reexamine how we as a country start dealing with an issue that we have seldom, if ever, had to face: how do we increase the working-age population to propel the growth of our economy and generate the fiscal resources to address our common needs and increase the rate of growth in our economy?

The disruption caused by the twins of the workers gap and the age demographic penalties should be our primary focus of our national policy debate.

Paradoxes on Population Growth

The answer to the question of growing this labor force confronts several of the most difficult paradoxes that we face. Many argue that there are too many people on Earth already and that any increase in population, even if needed to support economic growth and maintain fiscal sustainability, will continue to put more pressure on depleted or depleting natural resources. Increasing population using any strategy is not acceptable to zero population growth supporters. Paul Ehrlich's *The Population Bomb*[10] started this drumbeat in the 1970s, and it has been beating ever since. Researchers, politicians, and business leaders worldwide have responded to this challenge by developing a new approach to managing the Earth's resources— *sustainable development*. The principles of this approach, discussed in the previous chapter, are the same as increasing returns on investment (ROI) in the private sector and fiscal sustainability in the public sector.[11]

The climate change debate, in which many argue that humans are the main reason for the acceleration of the carbon dioxide emissions, has only added fuel to the fire. Growth of any kind, people and economic, is not a desired outcome. The principles of sustainability in both fiscal and environmental decision making provide a vehicle for working around this issue. The insights gained from common-pool resource management and the concepts being developed in the Fiscal Sustainability Index, with support from the Lincoln Institute for Land Policy (discussed in Chapter 11), provide a way to make allocation of resources and growth sustainable. If decisions on growth and allocation of resources are oriented toward the goals of economic growth, environmental and fiscal sustainability, there is a pathway to address this paradox.

Another paradox is that technology will be able to replace humans not only in production processes but also in other dimensions of economic activity. We will not need additional workers to propel our economies forward. Machines, robots, driverless cars, and many new inventions will make human participation obsolete not only in manufacturing but also in the service industries. So don't worry about the declining workforce and working age populaton.

Some observations about this paradox: For the past two decades, the period of the new economy and the wave of technology advances, productivity growth in our economy has been declining, not increasing although in this book I argue that if the demographic penalties are included, productivity would be higher. The gestation period of technology may need to be longer is often the reply to these observations, while others suggest new technologies are supplemental to human activity and create new types of jobs to support the work. The more fundamental problem with this pathway is that for economies to work, they need workers earning incomes who spend money on consuming both market and public goods—the Henry Ford principle of paying workers enough to buy his car. And workers come from the pool of working-age population.

This paradox raises even more profound questions about the real meaning of work. Pope Francis in his recent encyclical, *Laudato Si': On Care for Our Common Home*, provides us with new insights on the value of work that amplify the importance of the worker who is the consumer and, in the context of this book, the decision maker in the economic order that is evolving:

> We were created with a vocation to work. The goal should not be that technological progress increasingly replaces human work, for this would be detrimental to humanity. Work is a necessity, part of the meaning of life on this earth, a path to growth, human development and personal fulfillment. Helping the poor financially must always be a provisional solution in the face of pressing needs. The broader objective should always be to allow them

a dignified life through work. Yet the orientation of the economy has favored a kind of technological progress in which laying off workers and replacing them with machines reduce the costs of production. This is yet another way in which we can end up working against ourselves. The loss of jobs also has a negative impact on the economy "through the progressive erosion of social capital: the network of relationships of trust, dependability, and respect for rules, all of which are indispensable for any form of civil coexistence" [note deleted]. In other words, "human costs always include economic costs, and economic dysfunctions always involve human costs." [note deleted][12]

Work not only enables us to be economic actors but also is a pathway for human development, dignity, and a cornerstone for a civil and responsible society. This understanding of work suggests that technology must support the development of the individual, the income earner, the consumer, the taxpayer, and the decision maker in an ever-changing world.

The political paradox, even more volatile today than the overpopulation and technology issues, is too many people and too few jobs so we simply cannot have any more immigrants—we do not need any more people. There simply are not enough opportunities to go around. We have too many people and not enough jobs for the existing domestic population. Immigration is seen as driving wages down, with the perception that immigrants will work for less income and take jobs away from the domestic-born population. Another perception is that immigrants arrive, particularly refugees, fleeing political and economic conditions, needing education and other services that strain our currently pressed public sector. Finally, the experiences with domestic terrorism involving immigrant populations are creating a new wave of xenophobia in the United States and other developed countries. A day hardly goes by when there is not a media story in our 24/7 news cycle amplifying these claims that reached a flash point with the Brexit vote in Great Britain and played a major role in the election of Donald Trump in the 2016 presidential cycle. The political backlash is making immigration a difficult chapter in politics around the world.

On the other hand, without immigration we would not have a sufficient working-age population to sustain the meager growth we do have—the political paradox that more fully describes the underbelly of the political debate in our country. In the United States, the growth of the foreign-born working-age population in the last 15 years is twice the rate of the domestic-born working-age population.[13] So we have not only relied on immigrants to propel our economy but also to increase our working-age population.

If we do not find a way to increase our working-age population, the GDP growth rate of 1.8 percent of the past 15 years could very well be the best of times over the ensuring decades. In light of the long-term demographic penalties that will increase exponentially over the next several decades, and the workers' gap that will continue to act as a drag, our economic growth could be substantially lower than projected.

Finally, many of the policy tools to deal with growth are of questionable value in light of the magnitude of the demographic twin dampers of the workers' gap and the demographic age penalties. The fast-growing national debt makes fiscal policy an unlikely path; and monetary policy has shown over the past eight years that it can stabilize a crisis, but it has had difficulties stimulating growth when facing demographic headwinds. The time may be approaching to find ways to deal with these paradoxes of growth, both real and political.

Paradoxical Success Strategies

Like most paradoxes, the ones just described have no easy solutions, only possible strategies that can be used, in an attempt to work around what seems impossible. One workaround is to minimize the environmental footprint created by people that are here by maximizing the human development potential of work by all Americans. Stated very simply, no person is disposable. The workaround is to develop a strategy to bring into the working population individuals who historically were not considered workers, who have dropped out for multiple reasons, or who have been excluded. Include people of working age who have been considered, from a work perspective, "disposable." Include those outside the working-age population who are over 65. Include workers who have been structurally unemployed for so long they have dropped out of the labor force. Include those who have a prison record, those who may have a learning or physical disability. And, yes, include those who are in the United States illegally. Many of these populations receive transfer payments from the government and are not part of the labor force, but could be, with a coordinated effort, they could be.

We now have a collective reason to put these populations front and center and deal with them for our own sake. We need to get as many people as possible into the working-age population pool. We could follow the insights of Pope Francis on work as a human development initiative, in which work, in addition to being the major contributor to growth in the economy, provides a new way of dealing with cohesion in civil society and addresses dysfunctions that we observe in our country. Bringing everyone into the working-age population grows our economy, brings more tax dollars to the table and reduces demands on stressed fiscal resources.

Focusing on using "no one is disposable" through work as the strategy allows us to address multiple issues simultaneously. First, it grows the economy by adding to our working-age population, thus increasing the number of economic actors contributing in many ways to the economy. The view that "This is all well and good, but where will the jobs come from?" is a static view of economic growth. It assumes away the dynamic energy of more people involved in economic activity. Along the way it provides the vehicle for addressing social cohesion and increases in the civil society by allowing people to do something for others. These reciprocal economic relations can have positive social impacts on the operation of our society and give us a reason to deal with social issues that have been frustrating us for decades. Finally, it provides a way of dealing with governmental fiscal issues that seem insolvable. The insights of Pope Francis are more helpful now than ever, giving us a new way of thinking about issues that we tried to address for decades. Finally, it increases growth and not our environmental footprint.

3-D Strategies for Human Development: The Art of the Possible

The rules of the game that we developed for participation in the economy were for a different time when the economic base was different and with a different set of technologies and different economic needs. The 3-D approach discussed in earlier chapters is a new approach. It puts our organizations together in a new way to address our population paradoxes. With this approach, we can rebuild our economic base and our infrastructure, assuring the sustainability of the built environment and the fiscal environment using common-pool management. Then by effectively enrolling many more of our existing people in our working population, we can address many of our social pathologies and contribute to reducing our public fiscal deficiencies.

The following are new ways of thinking about America's working-age population using this approach.

Changing the path of economic development has to start with people. People will cause the change. The approach and principles of North, discussed in earlier chapters, of changing the rules of how organizations work together to chart a new path is applicable to developing our people. The goal is to maximize human capital by developing every person so that no one is disposed or left out. The economic return is clear: more economic growth, more tax revenue, and more social cohesion and elimination of social dysfunction costs and environmental externalities are achieved by eliminating the hidden twins.

"Partnerships of Progress"

Some initiatives are easy to do and have already begun. Many over the age of 65 are working, either because they did not save enough for retirement or their retirement investments were reduced during the Great Recession. Many retirees find new employment because they enjoy the fulfillment of working and doing something for others. Given the large number of boomers who are retiring each day, the redirection of retirees to new less physical employment opportunities could provide new pathways for 35 million retirees over the next 20 years. Many companies in a variety of industries are already employing older workers, particularly in the retail sector. We are reading stories almost daily of individuals who retire and move on to their next act, particularly in the world of nonprofits. Christopher Farrell writes about this phenomenon in an article entitled "Nonprofit Work Lets Retirees Pursue Passions and Pay." Employment in nonprofits has increased from 10.5 million jobs in 2007 to 11.4 million jobs in 2012. This article tells the stories of Archie Elam, an army career officer in Stamford, Connecticut, who is now a nonprofit executive; and Catherine Foley, a public affairs officers in Arizona, who retired to run an arts nonprofit. In addition to offering paid work, nonprofits provide opportunities for volunteering.[14]

The flexibility of nonprofits and partnerships with the public sector is creating the largest platform for the next act in America. Rejuvenating our human capital is the key to our economic growth. The examples of successful economic development experiments that are occurring across the country show how "no one is disposable" can be possible.

The flexibility of nonprofits to form partnerships with both the public and private sectors is creating the largest platform for the next act in America. Rejuvenating our human capital is the key to our economic growth. The examples of successful economic development experiments that are occurring across the country show how everyone matters and "no one is disposable" can be possible. In Los Angeles, the New Village Girls Academy, a charter school in the Los Angeles Unified School District, is successfully educating, each year, more than 120 young women with multiple indicators that usually predict failure: unwed mothers, at least 40 percent are pregnant or parenting; 20 percent are or have been in the juvenile justice system; 60 percent start New Village years behind grade and competency levels; all are below the poverty line and were previously in the Los Angeles County penal system. Graduates matriculate with a high school diploma. The most promising accomplishment of the school is that the graduates have the same matriculation performance as other high school students in the district. While it is taking them more than four years to graduate because many are working to support themselves and their children, a growing number of New Village grads enroll and stay in college: 50 percent of the class of 2015 enrolled that fall, continued in 2016 and were joined by two more from their graduating class; 70 percent of the 2016 class enrolled in college that September. New Village graduates attend mainly California State University, and junior colleges. Some are in California universities including Berkeley and UCLA, and several are in private universities, including Howard. Seventy to eighty percent continue their education past high school with many attending universities.

Success with this high-risk population is made possible by "partnerships through progress" approaches. New Village Girls Academy has key community partners, such as the partnership between the school and the Order of Saint Anne's, a home for unwed mothers, a social service agency for at-risk, pregnant and/or parenting young women and their children, on whose campus the school is located; the Los Angeles County Juvenile System; and the Foster Child Department. The purpose of the partnership is to meet the needs of these students. The New Village Board of the charter school not only serves as stewards for the school, but they also raise significant amounts of funds each year, thirty percent of the budget, with Los Angeles Unified providing the remainder through average daily attendance (ADA) funding. But the key to New Village educational success is the partnership with multiple foundations and organizations that have teamed to provide services and support. Big Picture Learning, a nonprofit, provided assistance in designing a curriculum that focuses on individualized student guidance learning, internships in the community and mentoring, essential for a student population that demands flexibility. Another nonprofit, the Young Policy Institute, provides athletic after school programs including athletics assistance, and mentoring, coinciding with internships and employment. St. John's Well Child and Family Center provides health care, and the David Lynch Foster Foundation, a nonprofit, provides the daily psychological assistance including a meditation program, core parts of the New Village Wellness Program and other counseling services to assist in the personal readjustment process. Foundation and individual funding provides a vice principal who directs the Wellness Program, a college counselor, and a school psychologist. Finally, a private foundation of a board member, the Bogen Family Foundation, is providing living quarters for additional young mothers along with a day care center—also on the campus. What has been created is a world of partnerships between public agencies, nonprofits, public and private; all aimed at one goal, to give these young women, mothers, and their children, a second chance. Our working-age population can be enhanced. This is truly the art of the possible.[15]

What has been created is a world of partnerships between public agencies, nonprofits, public and private, all aimed at one goal: to give these young mothers and their children a second chance. This is the essence of the American dream. It worked for our forefathers and it will work for future generations. When you consider the costs of warehousing this population in the penal system, sending their children off to foster homes, and the societal dysfunction and costs that this creates over a long time, we begin to see what Pope Francis is suggesting. Our working-age population can be enhanced and the social dysfunction that has a high cost can be averted. Most importantly the civil society that John Gardner in *On Leadership* wrote about, is the key to building community and creating social cohesions.[16] We wonder how we are going to deal with the increasing social dysfunctionality of our times. The New Village Academy shows the art of the possible, that it can be done. We need our working-age population to be productive. The cost savings from declining societal dysfunction over time will finance the restoration process and then some. Organizing ourselves in a 3-D set of relationships is the key to expanding the art of the possible. The network institutional design of organizations in our society enables us to address the greatest need we face in our country and our communites today, human development of all our population- no one is disposable.

Financial reasons for working longer, personal fulfillment reasons for working after retirement, and work having a broader meaning than economic are all informal rule changes that might cause us to look at changing the formal rules of the game. Take the setting of the retirement age that occurred during an agricultural and manufacturing era. The postmodern, information era is different and suggests that it is time to look again at retirement and pension ages. There is already a growing change in the informal rules occurring: people are already working longer for personal development and fulfillment, and for financial reasons. If there is a collective understanding and preference for working longer, then formal rules become politically possible.

In the past, the politics surrounding these programs have been the third rail of politics. Recipients have opposed any change, and our leaders have been reluctant to propose one even though the Social Security account needs more financial contributions. The politics of the demographic penalty and the workers' gap suggests a new calculus in which we all need to re-up, work longer, and make new financial contributions that support growth in the country, which in return will provide returns to us— including income, creating a culture of interdependence in which we look out for one another, and work in ways that bring personal satisfaction and societal improvements.

Governments, at all levels, need to reexamine how they collectively relate to their constituents who are working not as dependents on government but rather interdependently to meet their needs and the needs of the nation. The levels of government need to change the way they relate, from the historic hierarchy of relationships, from federal to state and local and then to the people, the so-called layer cake. To meet individuals' goals and needs, we have to become a "partnership for progress" with one another, with other sectors particularly at the local levels, and with shared constituents. Through these partnerships, duplication in federal programs can be identified and policies have a chance of being successful to alter the programs. For example, there are three separate disability programs that need integration. Participation in one or more of the safety net programs can have tax implications for the working poor that become a disincentive to work. Even the Earned Income Tax Credit (EITC) has the same effect. Co-coordinating and integrating the multiple transfer programs through realignment at various levels of government was accomplished in the past and now needs to be updated with a new goal to develop our working-age population.[17] The formal rules of the game for our safety net and our pension programs will need to be changed to reinforce the emerging 3-D pathway of human development.

Undocumented Immigration

If no one is disposable, the most controversial political issue is undocumented immigration. The 2015 estimate is 11.3 million people,[18] with the majority of children born to parents who were not here legally. The issue is so difficult that it has divided Congress for decades and frustrated the administration of both Presidents Bush and Obama. The inability to deal with this issue has led to a resurgence of political orthodoxy that was the root cause of the Brexit vote in Great Britain and the recent 2016 presidential election. The presence of the workers' gap and the demographic age penalty provides a new way of looking at the issue. If we need more working-age population, the presence of this asset could help us find a workaround. The 3-D "Public Finance Authority" approach in the economic regions that are struggling to increase their growth could use this labor force population as an asset. The 3-D "partnerships for performance" to develop all our people and ensure no one is disposal will employ many to be successful. You might ask where will the resources come from? The savings from removing the dysfunctional behavior in our society as Pope Francis suggests is the answer. The example of the New Village Charter School is but one example. The operative element of this approach is looking at every person in our nation as an asset, not as a liability. By following this approach, we can achieve more economic growth and see fewer displaced and for-gotten people and a more cohesive civil society.

Strategies That Add to Our Population Footprint

All of these strategies are aimed at using the population that is in the country to add to our working-age population. Much can be achieved through this approach, but a shortfall will still continue, particularly in the short term. Encouraging immigration and increasing the fertility rate of women remain as viable strategies if we are willing to undertake the policies to work around the difficulties they continue to pose.

Policies that are common to both must address sustainability issues, so that the adverse effect of an added footprint does not erode our quality of life. The 3-D "Public Finance Authority" strategy for dealing with growth, infrastructure, and human development, described in Chapter 12, provides a way of paying for the needed investments. More important, it reengages people as the major decision makers and leaders in making things happen. If we are involved in the decision making, we are more apt to develop confidence and trust in the solution. We can overcome the reasons why we dispose of so many people.

Immigration

The growth forecast used in this book, the 2014 Census Forecast, assumes immigration but at lower rates. The first question is, can we continue to evolve the economic strategy, as described in Chapter 11, so that more opportunities are provided? We have made progress in the past several years, and there is no reason with our global competitive advantages of our political system and our population we can be successful. We just have to use all of our population. Can an increase in the working-age population create human development synergy that accelerates development of employment opportunities? If so, we can change the growth rate of the country.

Next, can we use America's greatest strengths, our system of government, and our working-age population to continue to attract skilled workers who can advance 21st -century industries? Our universities, the envy of the world, are attracting the best from around the world. Recent accounts of the number of foreign students enrolled in our nations educational institutions are one million students.[19] Enabling these educated students to add to our nation's productivity. Rather than send them away upon graduation, we should develop rules of the game so that when they come, they are on a pathway to stay here.

Increasing the Fertility Rate

Decisions to form households, to have and raise children, to provide for their education and development, and regeneration of the human capital needed to continue to grow the economy are the most important decision that individuals will make. This is the most basic individual choice that we make. Given the impact of the demographic penalty described in this book, it is also the most important. Moreover, it is a difficult decision to influence and is not directed by government; witness China's problems in trying to change its one-child policy.

What does alter the fertility rate? Why was there a birth rate explosion after World War II and the reemergence of fertility increase after the Great Depression? Was it the calming influence of the peace settlement, or the country's growth policies, or the advances in our educational system? Probably all of these and more are reasons, including the desire to rebuild after several decades of disruptive events such as war and a depression.

We have had 15 years of difficulties caused by transformations and recessions. Are we seeing the same forces beginning to well up again, as described in the work of the Fallows and Storper, and illustrated by the new nonprofit partnership for progress initiatives that are attracting so many of our workers, young and old? Are the American people developing a new collective sense of working together? New ways to build and finance our local communities and new partnerships that focus on human development and that can be used to increase the birth rate? Only a few examples are provided in this chapter, which is deserving of its own book. Are new initiatives changing how we work in our communities to create economic opportunity, employment, and new pathways to grow the economy? Will the logistics supply chain regions create new links between the large urban regions and the exurbia and rural portion of these new megaregions? We are the answers to these questions through our individual and collective actions. The answers will define our economy and determine whether "We the People" are the architects of "We the Economy."

Notes

1. These calculations are derived from Table 5.1, "U.S. Population Changes, 1980–2035" in Chapter 5 which show the changes in population growth in each decade over the past 35 years and the U.S. Census prediction the next two decades.

2. This material is derived from tables in Chapters 3 and 4.

3. Bureau of Labor Statistics, National Compensation Survey, 2016, https:// www.google.com/search?q=Bureau+of+Labor+Statistics+Sources+of+income+s eries%2C2016&oq=Bureau&aqs=chrome.1.69i57j69i59j69i61l3.5.

4. Shelley K. Irving and Tracy A. Loveless, *Dynamics of Economic Well-Being: Participation in Government Programs 2009–2012: Who Gets Assistance?* (Washington, D.C.: Census Bureau, May 2015), https://www.census.gov/content/dam /Census/library/publications/2015/demo/p70-141.pdf.

5. Peter Wagner and Bernadette Rabuy, "Mass Incarceration: The Whole Pie 2016," *Prison Policy Initiative*, March 14, 2016, http://www.prisonpolicy.org/reports/ pie2016.html/.

6. Jeremy Travis, Bruce Western, and Steve Redburn, *The Growth of Incarcerations in the United States: Exploring Causes and Consequences, of Incarcerations* (Washington, D.C.: National Research Council, 2014), http://www.nap.edu/catalog /18613/the-growth-of-incarceration-in-the-united-states-exploring-causes.

7. Matthew Friedman, "Just Facts: As Many Americans Have Criminal Records as College Diplomas," Report, Brennan Center for Justice, November 28, 2015.

8. Binyamin Appelbaum, "Out of Trouble, but Criminal Records Keep Men Out of Work," *New York Times*, February, 28, 2015, http://www.nytimes.com /2015/03/01/business/out-of-trouble-but-criminal-records-keep-men-out-of -work.html?_r=0.

9. Nicholas Eberstadt, *Men without Work: America's Invisible Crisis* (West Conshohocken, PA: Templeton, 2016), p. 149.

10. Paul Ehrlich, *The Population Bomb* (New York: Ballantine Books, 1968).

11. Richard F. Callahan and Mark A. Pisano, "Aligning Fiscal and Environmental Sustainability," in Daniel Mazmanian and Hilda Blanco (Eds.), *Elgar Companion to Sustainable Cities: Strategies, Methods and Outlook* (Cheltenham, U.K.: Elgar, 2014).

12. Pope Francis, *Laudato Si': On Care for Our Common Home* (Vatican City: Vatican Press, May 24, 2015).

13. U.S. Census Forecast, 2014.

14. Christopher Farrell, "Nonprofit Work Lets Retirees Pursue Passions and Pay," *New York Times*, June 24, 2016, http://www.nytimes.com/2016/06/25/your -money/nonprofit-work-after-retirement-maybe-you-can-make-it-pay.html?_r=0.

15. Information derived from the website of New Village Partners, site visit, and discussion with board members, particularly Belinda Walker and staff.

16. John W. Gardner, *On Leadership* (New York: Free Press, 1990).

17. The framework for this "partnership for progress" approach is framed by Joe Wholey, who is suggesting new partnerships among federal agencies with state and local organizations, both public and nonprofits. Barry VanLare is suggesting a new alignment among the levels of government. These "memos" are for the leaders of the transition in government to occur in 2017.

18. Jeffery S. Passel and D'Vera Cohen, "Unauthorized Undocumented Immigrants Stable for Half a Decade," Pew Center for Research, July 22, 2015.

19. Douglas Belkin and Te-Ping Chen, "Foreign Students Hit Record," *The Wall Street Journal*, November, 14, 2016.

CHAPTER FOURTEEN

Conclusion

"Human beings cannot be expected to feel responsibility for the world unless, at the same time, their unique capacities of knowledge, will, freedom and responsibility are recognized and valued."

—Pope Francis[1]

The painting-by-numbers approach to the portrait of the American economy uses actual people as the assumption and how we organize ourselves as the composition. It gives us a different view of our future than policy forecasts based on models and the policy pronouncements of our government and business leaders. This view is based on who we are, how we age and grow, and the decisions that we make during our lives. This is our story of the American economy. This is what we contribute to and need from our political process. The results are surprising; at times startling, and prompt a change in how we make decisions about our future.

This picture of America describes the sum of the individual decisions that we make. It is our demographic makeup and what we do, as captured by the decisions we actually made, that contributed to the economy and politics in the past three decades. Based on this behavior, we can envision what could happen in the next three decades with the collective "us" as the decision maker. The discussion of the future is not a forecast or a predication. It is rather a baseline indicator of what could happen if we do not intervene and change the path we are currently following that does not seem to be working. The actual performance of growth in GDP, income, and taxes paid over the past 15 years is less than half the percentage increases of the previous three decades. We should not need more performance evaluations and data to know that something fundamental has changed. We need to change course. We need to do something different.

What made these paintings possible is the aggregation of the 324 million data points of our behavior from 1984 to date, made possible by the existence of big data. The analytic methods used to make sense of this data are much like George Orwell's *1984*, except that "big brother and the specter of government" are not the observer; rather, big data enables "us" to be the observers. The picture from this data is not an image on a cave that Plato mused about, but rather evidence to inform a Socratic thought process in order to develop wisdom about our future.

The "Workers' Gap" Is Economics' Driving Force

The most important conclusions from this data are summarized by two words: workers' gap. This economic condition arises when the availability of working-age people is not enough to stimulate the economy. Recall the riddle about Recession in the introduction. The bull-headed monster wants to know what is the one element that no economy can exist without but is shrinking in the wrong place in the United States? If you answered money, sorry—economies have existed without money (barter system), and the United States has more cash than it ever has before. The correct answer is a growing *working-age population*. We are simply not growing enough individuals to fuel a growing, business-creating, innovating, working, consuming, tax-paying labor force. We need a supply of working age to drive the economy. A simple comparison of the 57 million working age population growth of the past three decades with 25 million growth that we are expecting is evidence that "Recession" has given us the insight we need to make America great again. To fully understand our challenge add to this the 12 million working age who have opted out and the concern about the 11.3 not legally here.

Since we have benefitted from the big demographic databases that have been developed in recent decades, one can only wonder whether the concept of the "liquidity Trap," a concept developed by John Maynard Keynes in 1937 to describe the circumstance when an oversupply of capital cannot stimulate economic growth, wasn't actually influenced by this demographic shortage. Since the big data world with all our analytical capacity had not yet arrived when Keynes developed this observation we can only speculate. Many of the demographic characteristics of today were present then-restrictions on immigration and declining fertility rates. Without growth in the supply of working-age population there is not enough worker formation to create a healthy labor market. Labor and work include not just those who labor in the factory or the field, but all the human energy, drive, and sweat that galvanizes an economy. Workers and work become the foundation that not only stimulates and increases income, consumption, and taxes paid, but also enables development of human dignity and provides a stabilizing force to a civil society. Pope Francis has recently discussed this latter insight on work. Without growth in work and workers, our economy falls into a workers' trap that dampens economic activity, slows growth in the economy, and does not adequately use the liquidity that has been amply provided through our monetary policy. The workers gap behaves like a trap. This is a condition where the economy begins to stall and crawl. For a nation whose very culture is based on dynamic growth, this is a perplexing and disturbing condition.

Making matters worse, the aging of our population is now creating a large number of individuals who have also reached the stage of their lives where income, consumption, and taxes paid also declines. Actually, that we are aging so well, with many able to enjoy the fruits of their labor, is a very good sign. But from the perspective of our economy, the combination of not enough workers and large increases in the aging population is creating a demographic age penalty that is a drag on the economy. Together, the demographic twins of the workers' gap and the demographic penalty are shaping up to be anchor holding back the economy.

Our big-data view of the economy allows a quantification of the workers' gap as well as the demographic penalty and its converse, the demographic age bonus—a condition that arises when the working-age population increases substantially. The demographic bonus arises when the supply of workers increases and the increases in their income are aggregated, creating an unexpected and unforecasted amount of income. The demographic penalty is the reverse: fewer workers making less, and many more retirees making less, again, all aggregated. The magnitude of these aggregations is extremely large and surprising. Since the millennium, the sum of these penalties were: GDP-$3.34 trillion, Income—$2.27 trillion, Consumption—$1.12 trillion, and Taxes Paid—$2.27. They will steadily increase over the next two decades to GDP-$28 trillion, Income—$24.5 trillion, Consumption-$11.9 and Taxes Paid—$10.3 trillion (Constant 2015 dollars). Prior to the millennium, the demographic age bonus helped create the Goldilocks economy in the 1990s. Because the penalty is in the form of unrealized income, consumption, and taxes paid, our national income accounts do not measure them. But the results—of lower GDP, consumption, and tax revenue growth of almost 50 percent over the first 15 years of this century—tell us that they are having a significant impact. They tell us that the economic course we following is not working.

These impacts are so large and impact so many in America that they are now causing reverberations in our political processes that are jarring and unsettling. Listen to what we heard in the 2016 presidential campaign: a lack of opportunity, no wage increases, too many immigrants, and global trade stealing American jobs. Unfortunately, because of the stealth nature of the workers' gap and related issues, many of the proposed solutions put forth by the candidates targeted the wrong problems, and they are likely to have unintended consequences that will actually make things worse.

The second half of the book suggests ways of correcting for these demographic impacts. First, make demographics transparent in our economic analysis at all levels of government and in our academic and business forecasting. Demographics has to be more than hidden assumptions. The first step is to fully understand and make transparent the stealth twins: workers' gap and demographic age penalty. This is accomplished by making the long-term forecasting work of the CBO and GAO visible and by creating capacity in our states, regions, and businesses. Using big data from the large Census surveys of population and economic behavior, we can describe our collective decisions in the context of what really did happen between 1984 and today. This enables us to test the validity of our observations and our policy decisions in the 40-plus years from 1984 to 2016. From this analysis, we can learn whether our leaders were listening to us—not our protests and anger, but our aggregate behavior and decisions as captured by the big-data surveys and included in the aggregation analysis.

In this new form of public participation, we can learn whether good decisions were made when mapped against our collective decisions. This comparison helps us understand whether our decisions were wise or just plain lucky) e.g., Reagan and Clinton on their tax cut strategies and the synergy of the demographic bonus that our individual decisions created) or unlucky, (e.g., their timing was bad) Bush's and Obama's corrective course has been mired in the demographic penalty that started in 2001, continues to today, and will only get worse if our path is not altered.

Power of Collective Individual Choice

Even more important than the evidence we gathered from the painting and mapping process is the realization of the significance of our collective and individual decisions. For example, individual decisions to have children grows our working-age population; individual decisions to pick up and move around the country and the world, increase in-migration (movement around the country) and immigration (movement from abroad) to the United States; decisions to improve our well-being extends life; decisions on what products to buy increases or decreases trade; and so on. The results of our individual decisions, because of their aggregated size, actually can and did swamp the policy actions of our presidents, Congress, and the Federal Reserve. The calculations of the demographic bonuses and penalties in this book, granted they are the result of sensitivity analysis comparisons, are significantly effecting the monetary and fiscal decisions of our policy makers. The demographic bonus impacts in the Reagan and Clinton explain the effectiveness of the policy actions taken. The penalties of today are of a magnitude that they are frustrating the efforts of contemporary policy makers.

The collective choices we are making are not reflected in the policies decision makers are adopting. This disconnect has arisen because the results of our collective choices are not transparent, understood, and incorporated into the country's decision-making processes. This disconnect is now becoming apparent. It is having significant impacts on U.S. economic policy and politics, creating uncertainty about our future. From the events of the day, one might characterize our politics as dysfunctional and our economy as enigmatic. Until public participation is fundamentally changed to capture the results of collective choice decision making (i.e., taking our collective actions and including them in the actual analytics that our policy makers use), this disconnect will continue. Chapter 9 makes suggestions on the steps that can be taken to make our demographic economic decision making part of the policy process.

A New 3-D Economic and Political Base

From this work, a new pathway could be created that would change what could happen in the future by changing the formal rules of the game, using the framework of Douglass C. North. The evidence-based approach of this book provides information helpful to understanding North's values and informal rules, which could provide the basis for formal legislative designs and an institutional framework. Given the uncertainty of contemporary economics and politics, it could serve as a useful pathway.

Individual choice and decision making take on even more importance given the emergence of the information revolution and the communication technologies that have made them ubiquitous. Whenever governments attempt to corral this revolution, the IT world seems to find a way around the restriction. In the United States, not enough can be said about the power and importance of our collective individual decisions made possible by the freedoms that our governmental structure and processes have created. Our system of checks and balances and our decentralized approach to democracy not only encourage the power of collective individual choice but also accelerate its spread.

Out of this freedom emerged the liberating results of the innovations that are powering the world's economic future: information technologies, both hardware and software; and social networks and collaborative programs that support decentralized, distributive, and diverse problem solving. This is the toolkit that can be used to rebuild our economy and the provision of market goods. It also provides us the means to regenerate our public goods and our governance system. Chapters 10 and 11 outline the principles behind regenerating our economic base while maintaining fiscal and environmental sustainability. These chapters illustrate how new rules of the game, the theories of Douglass C. North, and the common-pool resource management theories of Elinor Ostrom can be used to reimagine and refine our economic and political systems. The focus of both chapters is on the importance of flexible, integrative systems that are predicated on reciprocal relationships with feedback and accountability that allow individuals to exercise their talents to be innovative, creative, and accountable.

What Can Be Done to Alter the Workers' Trap?

Central to this approach to economic development and governance is the "choice explosion" that is occurring in the United States, described by David Brooks in the *New York Times*[2]: "Americans now have more choices over more things than any other culture in human history." The challenge is to make moral decisions that consider the impact on other parts of the economic and political system. New formal rules of the game will enable us to move from a political world of dependence to a world of interdependence. The governance suggestions of these chapters are designed to achieve interdependence in our personal decision making that takes into account the reciprocal impact on others and on us. Geoff Mulgan, in *Connexity: How to Live in a Connected World*, describes how we move from a dependence-heavy world to interdependence when individual choice is guided by "moral" decision- makers who are concerned not only with themselves but also know their impacts on others.[3] Examples include making individual choices that enhance the size of our working-age population by increasing immigration, naturalizing those who work but are not here legally, increasing women's fertility rate, and utilizing all our working-age population by developing a "no one is disposable" approach to work. Pope Francis's articulation of work provides new meaning to our individual contribution to the economic system as the essence of human development and accountability. This is the foundation of a civil society. We need to make choices that are not dependent on a hierarchy (3-C) but rather in a (3-D) context where interdependence is possible. The governance suggestions in Part 2 of this book provide a vehicle for transformation.

The American People: Our Competitive Advantage

The common thread throughout this book is "We the People." As stated in the introduction, we need to look at the population not as an assumption but rather as the primary building block around which economic decisions are made. This is true not just for our firms but also for our national economy. The painting-by-numbers chapters formulate how to do this and quantify the results in order to address issues that are significant, difficult to resolve, and will last for a long time. The objective of the last chapter is to address the paradoxes that are limiting the size of our working-age population. Sorting out the "we versus immigrants" in the economic puzzle, the increase in the population versus a sustainable economy, the use of robots versus people, and growing our working-age population are the keys to our future. As recent history has shown, relying on fiscal and monetary policy alone, while necessary and important, is not sufficient and will lead to continuation down a path that is not working. The best—and maybe only—solution is to rely on our core strengths: our governmental system with the flexibility to solve the problems and unleash the innovation of "We the People" more effectively. The result is "We the Economy," *the solution to the Puzzle of the American Economy.*

Notes

1. Pope Francis, *Laudato Si': On Care for Our Common Home* (Vatican City: Vatican Press, May 24, 2015).
2. David Brooks, "The Choice Explosion," *New York Times*, May 3, 2016.
3. Geoff Mulgan, *Connexity: How to Live in a Connected World* (Boston: Harvard University Press, 1997), p. 236.

Bibliography

Adamy, Janet. "Low Birth Rate Poses Economic Challenge." *Wall Street Journal*, May 11, 2016, p. A2.

Anand, Greeta, and Jaeyeop Woo. "Asia Faces 'Missing Women' Problem." *Wall Street Journal*, November 27, 2015, p. A1.

Appelbaum, Binyamin. "Fed Raises Benchmark Interest Rate, Closing Chapter of U.S. Economic Recovery." *New York Times*, December 17, 2015, p. A1.

Appelbaum, Binyamin. "Lower Oil Prices Are Not Bringing Economic Gains: A Shift from the Past." *New York Times*, January 22, 2016, p. A1.

Barro, Josh. "Living Longer Is Great Except for Social Security." *New York Times*, November 17, 2015, p. A3.

Beinart, Philip. "Why America Is Moving Left." *The Atlantic*, January/February 2016, pp. 61–69.

Blinder, Alan S., and Mark Zandi, "Don't Look Back in Anger at Bailouts and Stimulus." *Wall Street Journal*, October 16, 2015, p. A13.

Blinder, Alan S., and Janet L. Yellen. *The Fabulous Decade: Macroeconomic Lessons from the 1990's* (New York: Century Foundation Press, 2001).

Blow, Charles M. "For Jobs, It's War." *New York Times*, September 17, 2011, p. A19.

Brooks, David. "The Choice Explosion." *New York Times*, May 3, 2016, p. A23.

Brooks, David. "The Post-Trump Era." *New York Times*, March 25, 2016, p. A23.

Brown, Ken. "As Debt Soars Again, No Need to Worry, Right?" *Wall Street Journal*, May 26, 2016, p. C1.

Buchholz, Todd G. *The Disunited States of America* (New York: Harper, 2016).

Bui, Quoctrung. "As More Older People Look for Work, They Are Put into 'Old Person Jobs.'" *New York Times*, August 18, 2016, p. A3.

Callahan, Richard F., and Mark Pisano. "Aligning Fiscal and Environmental Sustainability." *Elgar Companion to Sustainable Cities: Strategies, Methods and Outlook*, edited by Daniel A. Mazmanian and Hilda Blanco (Cheltenham, UK: Edward Elgar, 2014).

Chen, Te-Ping. "Chinese Face Hurdles to Baby Boom after Policy Shift." *Wall Street Journal*, October 31–November 1, 2015, p. 6.

Cimilluca, Dana, and Saumya Vaihampayan. "Global Stocks Sink on Fresh Growth Fears." *Wall Street Journal*, January 21, 2016, p. A1.

Cochrane, John H. "Ending America's Slow-Growth Tailspin." *Wall Street Journal*, May 3, 2016, p. A13.

Cohen, Patricia. "Plenty of Jobs, Too Few Workers." *New York Times*, January 29, 2016, p. B1.

Cost, Jay. "The Politics of Distrust." *Wall Street Journal*, October 17–18, 2015, pp. 1–2.

Das, Satyajit. *The Age of Stagnation: Why Perpetual Growth Is Unattainable and the Global Economy Is in Peril* (New York: Prometheus Books, 2016).

Davidson, Adam. "The Federal Reserve Affects Nearly Every Person on the Planet, but Almost No One Understands It—and That's by Design." *New York Times Magazine*, November 25, 2015, pp. 18–22.

Davidson, Kate. "Strong Jobs Report Clears Fed for Interest-Rate Liftoff." *Wall Street Journal*, December 5–6, 2015, p. A1.

Dendrinou, Viktoria. "Europe Sees Slower Growth." *Wall Street Journal*, November 6, 2015, p. A9.

Denison, Edward, assisted by Jean-Pierre Poullier. *Why Grow Rates Differ: Postwar Experience in Nine Western Countries* (Washington, D.C.: Brookings Institution, 1967).

Doar, Robert. "The Big but Hidden U.S. Jobs Problem." *Wall Street Journal*, January 12, 2016, p. A13.

Drucker, Peter F. *Management Challenges for the 21st Century* (New York: Harper Business Press, 1999).

Duara, Nigel, and Cindy Carcamo, "Balance Tips as More Exit U.S. for Mexico, Survey Finds." *Los Angeles Times*, November 20, 2015, p. A1.

El-Erian, Mohamed A. "The Fed Can't Save the Economy This Time." *New York Times*, January 22, 2016, p. A23.

Fallows, James, assisted by Deborah Fallows. "Can America Put Itself Back Together?" *The Atlantic*, March 2016, pp. 58–62.

Feldstein, Martin. "A Federal Reserve Oblivious to Its Effect on Financial Markets." *Wall Street Journal*, January 14, 2016, p. A13.

Feldstein, Martin. "The Uncounted Trillions in the Inequality Debate." *Wall Street Journal*, December 14, 2015, p. A17.

Fukuyama, Frances. *The Great Disruption: Human Nature and the Reconstitution of Social Order* (New York: Free Press, 1999).

Gabler, Neal. "The Secret Shame of the Middle Class." *The Atlantic*, May, 2016, pp. 52–63.

Galston, William A. "Why Trade Critics Are Getting Traction." *Wall Street Journal*, March 30, 2016, p. A11.

Geithner, Timothy F. *Stress Test: Reflections on Financial Crisis* (New York: Crown, 2014).

Giratikanon, Tome, Alicia Parlapiano. "Janet Yellen, on the Economy's Twists and Turns." *New York Times*, October 10, 2013, p. A19.

Gordon, Robert J. *The Rise and Fall of American Growth: The U.S. Standard of Living Since the Civil War* (Princeton, NJ: Princeton University Press, 2016).

Government Accountability Office. *State and Local Fiscal Report 2015.* Washington, D.C.: Author, January 2016. http://www.gao.gov/fiscal_outlook/st ate _local_fiscal_model/overview#t=2

Gramm, Phil, and Michael Solon. "Why This Recovery Is So Lousy." *Wall Street Journal*, August 4, 2016, p. A11.

Greenhouse, Steven. "The Mystery of the Vanishing Pay Raise." *New York Times*, November 1, 2015, Review, p. 3.

Harrison, David. "Budget Cuts Fuel Monetary Policy Clashes." *Wall Street Journal*, April 11, 2016, p. A2.

Harrison, David, and Heather Gillers. "Localities Opt for Les Debt over New Infrastructure." *Wall Street Journal*, August 8, 2016, p. A1.

Hilsenrath, Jon. "Fed Poised to Raise Rates in End of Era." *Wall Street Journal*, December 16, 2015, p. A1.

Hilsenrath, Jon, and Anna Louie Sussman. "Fed Doubts Grow 2015 Rate Hike." *Wall Street Journal*, October 15, 2015, p. A1.

Hinshaw, Drew. "African Baby Boom Brings Hope and Fear." *Wall Street Journal*, November 28–29, 2015, p. A1.

Hudson, Kris, and Jeffrey Sparshott. "Builders Suffer Labor Pains." *Wall Street Journal*, October 13, 2015, p. A2.

Ip, Gregg. "Older Demographic Poses Double Whammy for Economy." *Wall Street Journal*, August 4, 2016, p. A2.

Ip, Gregg. "Rewriting Recent Economic History." *Wall Street Journal*, June 2, 2016, p. A2.

Irwin, Neil. "A Guiding Principle That May Lead the Fed Astray." *New York Times*, October 2015, p. B1.

Irwin, Neil. "A Searching Fed Asks If It's Looking in the Right Places." *New York Times*, August 18, 2016, p. B1.

Irwin, Neil. "The Terrible, Wonderful, Inscrutable Economy." *New York Times*, November 3, 2015, p. B3.

Irwin, Neil. "Workers are Getting a Bit More of the Economic Pie." *New York Times*, The Upshot, May 6, 2016.

Jacobs, Jane. *Cities and the Wealth of Nations: Principles of Economic Life* (New York: Random House, 1984).

Khanna, Parag. "A New Map for America: Let's Move Past 50 States." *New York Times*, April 17, 2016, p. A1.

King, Neil. "Wages Cloud Economy's Role in Election." *Wall Street Journal*, February 9, 2016, p. A6.

Kondracke, Morton, and Matthew J. Slaughter. "Making the Case for Trade." *Wall Street Journal*, March 16, 2016, p. A15.

Krauss, Clifford. "Low Oil Prices and Tough Margins Pinch Results at Chevron and Exxon." *New York Times*, April 30, 2016, p. B5.

Krugman, Paul. "The Diabetic Economy." *New York Times*, May 2, 2016, p. A19.

Krugman, Paul. "Time to Borrow." *New York Times*, August 8, 2015, p. A 19.

Last, Jonathan V. *What to Expect When No One's Expecting: America's Coming Demographic Disaster* (New York: Encounter Books, 2014).

Lauter, David. "What People Think about Government." *Los Angeles Times*, November 24, 2015, p. A2.

Lee, Don. "Fears of U.S. Recession Are Growing." *Los Angeles Times*, January 28, 2016, p. Bl.

Levin, Yuval. "The Next Conservative Movement." *Wall Street Journal*, April 16–17, p. Cl.

Leibovich, Mark. "Inside Out." *New York Times Magazine*, March 3, 2016, p. 13.

Leonhardt, David. "We're Spent." *New York Times*, July 17, 2011, p. R6.

Leubsdorf, Ben. "No Easy Fix on Boosting Labor Force." *Wall Street Journal*, March 7, 2016, p. A2.

Leubsdorf, Ben. "Productivity Fall Imperils Growth." *Wall Street Journal*, August 10, 2016, p. Al.

Leubsdorf, Ben. "Recession's Fallout: Enduring Wage Scars." *Wall Street Journal*, May 10, 2016, p. Al.

Leubsdorf, Ben. "U.S. Comes to Grips with Slow Growth." *Wall Street Journal*, January 20, 2016, p. R4.

Leubsdorf, Ben, and Josh Mitchell. "Consumers Keeping Growth Afloat." *Wall Street Journal*, December 24, 2015, p. A2.

Lind, Michael. "Is There Too Much Democracy in America or Too Little?" *New York Times*, May 15, 2016, p. R6.

Lucia, Bill. "Do Americans Prefer State or Federal Power?" *Route Fifty-five Roadmap*, July 12, 2016.

McCloskey, Deidre N. "How the West Got Rich: And the Rest." *Wall Street Journal*, May 21–22, p. Cl.

McGurn, William. "Grow, Baby, Grow!" *Wall Street Journal*, February 16, 2016, p. A15.

Melloan, George. "Inattention-to-the-Deficit Disorder." *Wall Street Journal*, May 27, 2016, p. All.

Melloan, George. "Rising Global Debt and the Deflation Threat." *Wall Street Journal*, March 8, 2016, p. A13.

Meltzer, Allan H. "The Folly of Economic Short-Termism." *Wall Street Journal*, August 11, 2016, p. A15.

Morath, Eric. "U.S. in Weakest Recovery since '49." *Wall Street Journal*, July 30–31, p. Al.

Mulgan, Geoff. *Connexity: How to Live in a Connected World* (London: Random House, 1997).

Murray, Charles. "Trump's America." *Wall Street Journal*, February 13–14, p. Cl.

New York Times Editorial Board. "The Millions Who Are Just Getting By." *New York Times*, June 2, 2016, p. A20.

Nicas, Jack. "The Price You Pay Depends on Time of Day." *Wall Street Journal*, December 14, 2015, p. Bl.

North, Douglass C. *Institutions, Institutional Change and Economic Performance* (New York: Cambridge University Press, 1990).

Perry, Mark J. "The Economic Consensus on Trade." *Los Angeles Times*, March 16, 2016.

Peterson, Kyle. "When All Economics is Political." *Wall Street Journal*, May 14–15, p. A10.

Pisano, Mark. "Innovation in Planning and Funding Infrastructure Renewal: The London Experience." In *Innovation in the Public and Nonprofit Sectors,* edited by Patria de Lancer Julnes and Ed Gibson (New York: Routledge, 2016).

Porter, Eduardo. "The Debate about America's Best Days, and Future Prosperity." *New York Times*, January 20, 2016, p. B9.

Porter, Eduardo. "Reviving the Working Class without Building Walls." *New York Times*, March 9, 2016, p. B1.

Puzzanghera, Jim. "Can Brinkmanship Be Defused?" *Los Angeles Times*, October 19, 2015, p. A10.

Puzzanghera, Jim, and Don Lee. "A Long Rebound: Why the 7-year Economic Recovery Feels So Weak." *Los Angeles Times*, June 6, 2016, p. A12.

Rattner, Steven. "Jobless in the Lion's Den." *New York Times*, January 26, 2016, p. A25.

Rauch, Jonathan. "What's Ailing American Politics," *The Atlantic*, July/August 2016.

Regional Plan Association. *America 2015: A Prospectus.* New York: Author, September 2006.

Ridley, Matt. "The Myth of Basic Science." *Wall Street Journal*, October 24–25, 2015, p. C1.

Rosenberg, Nathan, and L.E. Birdzell, Jr. *How the West Grew Rich* (New York: Basic Books, 1984).

Schiff, Stacy. "Anger: An American History." *New York Times*, December 20, 2015, p. R5.

Schlesinger, Jacob M., and Alexander Martin. "Graying Japan Looks for a Silver Lining." *Wall Street Journal*, November 30, 2015, p. A1.

Schwartz, Nelson D. "The Fed Sees Mid-Income Jobs Finally Rebounding." *New York Times*, August 19, 2016, p. B1.

Schwartz, Nelson D. "Figures on U.S. Growth and Employment Tell Two Different Stories." *New York Times*, January 18, 2016, p. B3.

Schwartz, Nelson D. "Good Jobs, Goodbye." *New York Times*, March 20, 2016, p. B1.

Schwartz, Nelson D. "Two Sides to Economic Recovery: Growth Stall, While Jobs Soar." *New York Times*, April 12, 2016, p. B1.

Silver, Nate. *Why So Many Predictions Fail—but Some Don't* (New York: Penguin, 2012).

Sorkin, Andrew Ross. "Eight Years after the Crash: The Obama Recovery." *New York Times Magazine*, May 1, 2016, p. 54.

Sparshott, Jeffrey. "U.S. Growth Starts Year in Familiar Rut," *Wall Street Journal*, April 29, 2016, p. A1.

Stauffer, Robert F. "The Fed's Mismeasure of Inflation." *Wall Street Journal*, February 5, 2016, p. A 11.

Stephens, Bret. "The Return of the 1930s." *Wall Street Journal*, March 8, 2016, p. A11.

Stephens, Phil. "Politicians Are Paying the Bill for the Crash," *London Times*, December 18, 2015, p. A11.

Summers, Lawrence. "The Battle over the Budget Is the Wrong Fight." *London Times*, October 14, 2013, p. A13.

Sussman, Anna Louie. "Job Gains Ease Fed's Path." *Wall Street Journal*, November 7–8, 2015, p. A1.

Sussman, Anna Louie, and Josh Zumbrun, "'Gig' Economy Spreads Broadly." *Wall Street Journal*, March 26–27, 2016, p. A1.

Tau, Byron. "Arizona Race to Stress Immigration." *Wall Street Journal*," March 16, 2016, p. A9.

Timitaos, Nick. "Oil Rout Points to Broader Woes." *Wall Street Journal*, February 5, 2016, p. A2.

Torry, Harriet. "Declining Productivity Growth Poses Threat." *Wall Street Journal*, May 5, 2016, p. A2.

Tritch, Teresa. "Andy Groves Warning to Silicon Valley." *New York Times*, March, 26, 2016, p. A18.

U.S. Census Bureau. Population Survey. "What a Difference Four Years Makes: U.S. Population to Grow Slower over Next Five Decades." December 12, 2012, http://www.census.gov/population/projections.

Wall Street Journal Editorial Board. "Cracking Washington's Black Box." *Wall Street Journal*, April 4, 2016, p. A18.

Wall Street Journal Editorial Board. "The Deficit Rises Again." *Wall Street Journal*, January 26, 2016, p. A12.

Warsch, Kevin. "The Blame-Thy-Neighbor Economic Excuse." *Wall Street Journal*, April 29, 2016, p. A13.

Wessel, David. "Why It's Wrong to Dismiss the Deficit." *Wall Street Journal*, October 31, 2013, p. A4.

Zhong, Raymond. "A Blocked Path to Development." *Wall Street Journal*, November 25, 2015, p. A1.

Zumbrun, Josh. "Economists, CEOs: Recession Risk Rising." *Wall Street Journal*, February 12, 2016, p. A10.

Zumbrun, Josh. "Economists Sunnier Than Voters." *Wall Street Journal*, May 13, 2016, p. A2.

Zumbrun, Josh. "Forces That Opened Up Borders Show Signs of Sputtering." *Wall Street Journal*, April 4, 2016.

Zumbrun, Josh. "Global Malaise Spurs U.S. Growth Worries." *Wall Street Journal*, January 15, 2016, p. A1.

Index

About the Author

Mark A. Pisano is a professor of practice of public administration at the University of California, Sol Price School of Public Policy, the co-chair of the federal system panel of the National Academy of Public Administration, and a past executive director, for 32 years, of the Southern California Association of Governments.

www.ingramcontent.com/pod-product-compliance
Lightning Source LLC
Chambersburg PA
CBHW071418290326
41932CB00046B/2367